THE PRIESTLY OFFICE

A Theological Reflection

Avery Dulles, S.J.

PAULIST PRESS
New York • Mahwah, N.J.

Nihil Obstat: Francis J. McAree, S.T.D., Censor Librorum
Imprimatur: † Patrick Sheridan, D.D., Vicar General, Archdiocese of New York

Cover design by Moe Berman.

Library of Congress Cataloging-in-Publication Data

Dulles, Avery Robert. 1918–
    The priestly office: a theological reflection / Avery Dulles.
        p.   cm.
    Five lectures delivered at the Pastoral Institute for Clergy Formation, Seton Hall University, South Orange, N.J., June 25–26, 1996
    Includes bibliographical references and index.
    ISBN 0-8091-3716-X (alk. paper)
    1. Priests. 2. Catholic Church—Clergy. 3. Clergy—Office.
4. Priesthood. I. Title.
BX1912.D86 1997
262'.142—dc21   97-5289
                                                                      CIP

Published by Paulist Press
997 Macarthur Boulevard
Mahwah, New Jersey 07430

Printed and bound in the
United States of America

PREFACE

THE PRESENT BOOK CONSISTS OF five lectures delivered at the National Institute for Clergy Formation under the direction of Monsignor Andrew Cusack of Seton Hall University, South Orange, New Jersey, on June 25–26, 1996. It is offered as a modest introduction to the subject of ordained priesthood in the light of Vatican II and recent magisterial and theological teaching. In publishing these lectures the author wishes to express his gratitude to Monsignor Cusack for his leadership in directing this Institute, which has done so much for the education and renewal of priestly ministry over the past decade.

Avery Dulles, S.J.

CONTENTS

ABBREVIATIONS

Scripture

The abbreviations in the Revised Standard Version (New York: Oxford University Press, 1962), from which scripture quotations are taken, have been followed except where the contrary is indicated.

Documents of Vatican II

AA   Decree on the Apostolate of the Laity, *Apostolicam actuositatem*

AG   Decree on the Church's Missionary Activity, *Ad gentes*

DV   Dogmatic Constitution on Divine Revelation, *Dei verbum*

GS   Pastoral Constitution on the Church in the Modern World, *Gaudium et spes*

LG   Dogmatic Constitution on the Church, *Lumen gentium*

OT   Decree on Priestly Formation, *Optatam totius*

PO   Decree on Ministry and Life of Priests, *Presbyterorum ordinis*

SC   Constitution on the Sacred Liturgy, *Sacrosanctum concilium*

UR   Decree on Ecumenism, *Unitatis redintegratio*

Other

CDF Congregation for the Doctrine of the Faith

CIC Code of Can Law (1983)

CT John Paul II, Apostolic Exhortation on Catechesis in Our Time, *Catechesi tradendae* (1979)

DS *Enchiridion Symbolorum*, ed. H. Denzinger, rev. A. Schönmetzer (Freiburg: Herder, 1976)

EN Paul VI, Apostolic Exhortation on Evangelization in the Modern World, *Evangelii nuntiandi* (1975)

PDV John Paul II, Apostolic Exhortation on Priestly Formation, *Pastores dabo vobis* (1992)

RM John Paul II, Encyclical on the Church's Missionary Activity, *Redemptoris missio* (1990)

R&P John Paul II, Apostolic Exhortation on Penance and Reconciliation, *Reconciliatio et paenitentia* (1984)

ST Thomas Aquinas, *Summa theologiae*

I. THE PRIEST AND THE CHURCH

I T IS NOT UNCOMMON TODAY to speak of a crisis of priesthood in Western Europe and North America. Large-scale departures from the active ministry together with the catastrophic dip in vocations in some countries have given rise to concern in some cases bordering on alarm. The causes are doubtless complex, and I do not intend to analyze them in this volume. I believe, however, that one contributing cause has been the uncertainty about the role and identity of the priest arising from the introduction of new theological paradigms.

Historical Development

From patristic times through the middle of the twentieth century the Catholic Church has understood priesthood predominantly in sacral terms, as indeed priesthood has been understood in most religions including ancient Judaism. Priesthood, so conceived, revolves about temple worship and sacrifice. The priest, through sacred rites, mediates between human beings and the god or gods. Solidifying this tradition, the Council of Trent in its Decree on the Sacrament of Order defined the Catholic priesthood in terms of the powers to offer holy mass and to forgive sins (DS 1764).

This concept of priesthood was rejected by Protestantism as biblically unwarranted. Protestants understood Christ as having abolished the priestly office of Judaism and as being the sole priest of the New Covenant. All the baptized, they insisted, participated by equal right in the priestly office of Jesus. Protestant ministers, therefore, were not generally called priests.

After some centuries of Protestant-Catholic confrontation, Vatican II made an attempt to rethink the Catholic teaching from a standpoint that was at once more biblical, more ecumenical, and more contemporary. Without discarding the traditional concept of ministerial priesthood, it reworked that concept in light of the New Testament, partly, no doubt, in the hope of achieving a rapprochement with Protestantism. In so doing the council revived the concept of the common priesthood of the whole people of God, which had been practically dormant in Catholic theology. It depicted the ministerial priesthood as oriented in service toward the common priesthood of the baptized. The council likewise showed considerable restraint in applying priestly language to bishops and presbyters. It spoke of them as exercising a threefold office—prophetic, priestly, and royal. Priestly ministry, therefore, was only one dimension of an office that involved also the ministry of the word (the prophetic) and the ministry of the shepherd (the pastoral). In only a few texts did Vatican II designate bishops and presbyters by the title "priest" (Latin *sacerdos*, corresponding to the Greek *hiereus*).

Present Debates

This abrupt departure from a tradition of many centuries was bound to provoke some confusion, if not a crisis. The confusion was compounded by the work of avant-garde theologians, especially in the decade from 1965 to 1975. Not untypical was the book of Hans Küng, *Why Priests?* (published in English in 1972),[1] which called for an abolition of the term "priest" as applied to ministers of the church. According to the New Testament, Küng declared, all believers are priests. Instead of speaking of a ministerial or hierarchical priesthood in the church, he said, we should use functional terms such as "leader" and "presider." The term "hierarchy" should be abandoned. Although bishops and presbyters were the ordinary ministers of the eucharist and of the forgiveness of sins, these sacraments could in cases of urgent necessity be celebrated by charismatically gifted lay persons. Ministerial service, Küng contended, should be open to men and women. The commitment to ministry could be temporary rather than lifelong; there was no justification for the requirement that the ecclesiastical leaders be celibate.

Several of these positions of Küng were rejected by the Congregation for the Doctrine of the Faith (CDF) in the Declaration *Mysterium Ecclesiae* of June 24, 1973 and in a further declaration on Küng's work published on February 15, 1975.[2] Notwithstanding these condemnations, Edward Schillebeeckx followed suit by holding that in case of emergency a congregation could designate one of its own members to preside at the eucharist.[3] In his book entitled *Ministry: Leadership in the Community of Jesus Christ,* Schillebeeckx, like Küng, rejected the ontological understanding of the priestly character, which had been used as a basis for excluding the possibility that the nonordained could celebrate a valid eucharist. Not surprisingly, Schillebeeckx's book on ministry, like Küng's, was disapproved by the Roman Congregation for the Doctrine of the Faith in a letter to the world's bishops on the Ministry of the Eucharist (*"Sacerotium Ministeriale"*) of August 6, 1983.[4] This notification was followed by a letter to Father Schillebeeckx on June 13, 1984, asking him to signify his adherence to the teaching of the previous letter.[5]

In spite of the disapproval of their positions by the magisterium, theologians such as Küng and Schillebeeckx continued to be very influential with a broad public. Even today, many of the Catholic intelligentsia of Western Europe and the United States either reject the concept of ministerial priesthood or redefine it in ways that make it scarcely distinguishable from the concept of ministry in Protestant Congregationalism.

The Three Functions

The principal question before us in the present work will be whether we can propose a viable concept of ministerial priesthood that is coherent with the biblical data, with the Catholic tradition, and with the teaching of Vatican II. If so, can the concept hold its ground against radical theologians who would either reject the ordained priesthood altogether or reduce it to a merely functional ministry? I shall contend that it is possible and necessary to answer questions such as these in the affirmative. One source of difficulty is that Vatican II's concept of priesthood is made up of three disparate elements—the prophetic, the priestly, and the royal. Since the council many theologians have wondered whether a convincing rationale can be given for assigning all three functions to the same individual and calling that individual a priest. Even if the confection of the eucharist and the absolution from sins are reserved to priests, could not the functions of preaching and pastoral governance be taken over by others? Is priesthood to be reduced to the few functions that cannot be performed by anyone except bishops and presbyters? If the prophetic and pastoral tasks are no less important than the ritual, does priestly ministry still have the high significance and centrality traditionally attributed to it? Since the council there has been a considerable spread of opinion among theologians committed to defending the ministerial priesthood. Some, like Karl Rahner, take the ministry of the word as primary, and attempt to show that the fullness of this prophetic ministry involves the priestly and the pastoral as well. Others, like Otto Semmelroth and Joseph Lécuyer, begin with the ministry of worship and seek to integrate the prophetic and the pastoral ministries into it. Still a third school, represented by Walter Kasper, Hans Urs von Balthasar, and Jean Galot, takes the pastoral or shepherding function as primary, and derives the others from this. I shall attempt to set forth and critically evaluate these three positions in my second, third, and fourth chapters. In the present chapter I wish to develop some general considerations on priesthood using the Bible and the documents of the church as reference points.

Priesthood of Christ

It is often said that the priesthood of Christ should be the starting point for any Christian concept of priesthood. But the priestly status of Jesus Christ is not self-evident. Some theologians insist that Christ was a layman, and deny that he was a priest except in a metaphorical sense.

Sociologically speaking, Jesus was not a member of the Jewish priestly class. Nowhere in the gospels does he refer to himself as a priest, nor do others regard him as such. Except in the Letter to the Hebrews Jesus is never called a priest by any New Testament author. Hebrews does use priestly terminology, but some contend that its exalted concept of the priesthood of Christ delegitimates any other priesthood than his.

Granted the inspired and canonical status of the Letter to the Hebrews, the Christian theologian is justified in forming a concept of priesthood that applies at least to Jesus himself. Such a concept would involve being designated and empowered by God to offer prayers and sacrifice of praise, thanksgiving, and atonement on behalf of the whole people, thereby pleasing God and bringing divine benefits upon those for whom intercession is made. This concept does not demand the performance of any prescribed ritual or the use of any sacred location, such as a temple, but it retains the essentials of the concept of priesthood as found in Judaism and many other religions.

If the concept of priesthood in Hebrews is taken as a starting point, it becomes apparent that other New Testament authors such as Paul understand Jesus as a priestly figure, even though they do not use the term. They consider the death of Jesus on the cross to be a religious sacrifice. Indeed it becomes apparent that the idea of priesthood is pervasive in the New Testament descriptions of Jesus as the one who bore the sins of many and allowed his body to be broken and his blood poured forth on behalf of others.

Many New Testament authors describe Jesus as shepherd or pastor. The First Letter of Peter, for example, calls him the chief shepherd and also the lamb without spot or blemish, offered up for the sins of the world. These themes are extensively developed in the gospel of John, in which Jesus says of himself, "I am the good shepherd" (Jn 10:11). The sacrificial role is brought out in the statement immediately following: "The good shepherd lays down his life for the sheep" (ibid.). He does so in obedience to the Father's command, in order to win eternal life for the sheep committed to his care. In his priestly sacrifice the shepherd becomes the victim whose body and blood are true food and drink (Jn 6:53). He has a prophetic task as leader and teacher of the community, for the sheep hear his voice and follow him to the pastures of eternal life (Jn 10:27–28). Even the concept of kingship is not absent from the Johannine vision, for Jesus dies with the inscription on the cross, "King of the Jews" (Jn 19:19). He has told Pontius Pilate, "my kingship is not of this world" (Jn 18:36).

The category of priesthood, therefore, is biblically appropriate. While applying primarily to the prayer and sacrificial aspects of Jesus' ministry, it cannot be isolated from his prophetic and royal functions, which themselves take on priestly attributes. This conclusion is supported not only by the texts from Peter, Paul, and John, but also by the treatment of Jesus' priesthood in the Letter to the Hebrews. For the author of Hebrews, Christ's priesthood includes his divine appointment (5:4–6), his earthly supplication (5:7), his obedience to the Father (5:8), his sacrificial death (9:18), and his heavenly intercession (7:25). But the priestly ministry of Jesus is also prophetic, since he is the Son through whom God has spoken to us (1:2). Christ's priesthood, moreover, is royal, since it fulfills not the Aaronic or the Levitical but the priesthood of Melchizedek, the "king of righteousness" (7:2). Thanks to his sacrifice Christ the Priest is the mediator of the new covenant and the "great Shepherd" whom God has brought back from the dead to lead his flock (13:20). Thus the concept of priesthood in Hebrews goes beyond the merely cultic; it includes elements that have traditionally been reckoned under the prophetic and the royal.

The full concept of priesthood, enriched by these biblical data, centers on the ministry of reconciliation. The priest is a faithful emissary sent by God to rescue a whole people from death and to set them on the road to life. The mission involves self-offering and intercessory prayer for the sake of others. It also involves teaching and directing them in the ways of the new covenant with a view to their sanctification.

The Common Priesthood and the Ministerial

The biblical concept of priesthood applies to the whole covenant people. Already in the Old Testament, the nation of Israel is described as priestly insofar as it is consecrated to the service of God (Ex 19:6; Is 61:6). The New Testament, in the First Letter of Peter and in Revelation, applying this theme to the people of the New Covenant, calls the church "a royal priesthood, a holy nation, God's own people," chosen to "declare the wonderful deeds of him who called you out of darkness into his marvelous light" (1 Pet 2:9–10). According to the book of Revelation, those who have been redeemed by the blood of Christ are "a kingdom and priests to our God" (Rev 5:10; cf. 1:5–6).

This common priesthood of the whole church, conferred initially by the sacrament of baptism, enables the faithful to participate actively in the church's life of worship. It equips them to join in the offering of the eucharist and to receive other sacraments. The faithful also exercise their priesthood by the witness of a holy life, by self-denial, and by active charity, thereby participating in the prophetic and royal dimensions of Christ's priesthood.

Nowhere in the New Testament are the ministers of the New Covenant called "priests." So long as the temple worship continued in Jerusalem, the early Christians seem to have reserved the term for Jewish priests, but the church did have a special ministry. Initially this was the ministry of the Twelve. From the gospels one may learn that they were commissioned to evangelize the world (Mt 28:19), to baptize disciples (ibid.), to forgive sins (Lk 24:47; Jn 20:23), to celebrate the Lord's Supper in commemoration of Jesus (Lk 22:19–20; cf. 1 Cor 11:24–25), and to rule with authority in the community (Mt 18:17–18).

In the Acts and in the Epistles of the New Testament we see the apostles exercising these forms of ministry. Paul, though he sees his own ministry as consisting primarily in the proclamation of the gospel, describes that ministry in priestly terms. To the Romans he writes about "the grace given to me by God to be a minister of Christ Jesus in the priestly service of the gospel of God, so that the offering of the Gentiles may be acceptable, sanctified by the Holy Spirit" (Rom 15:15–16). In Philippians 2:17 he says that he rejoices "even if I am to be poured as a libation upon the sacrificial offering of your faith." He wishes to be regarded as an "ambassador of Christ" (2 Cor 5:20) and a "steward of the mysteries of God" (1 Cor 4:1). Appealing to his apostolic authority, he does not hesitate to give commands and lay down regulations for the communities he has founded, even at times imposing sanctions such as excommunication (1 Cor 5:5). Thus the royal dimension is not absent from Paul's priestly ministry, although that ministry was markedly prophetic.

In the later books of the New Testament we see the apostles handing their transmissible powers and functions to collaborators and successors. These writings make it clear that the authoritative ministry of the word and the rule of the churches were gradually entrusted to bishops and presbyters. In Paul's sermon at Miletus they are called overseers appointed by the Holy Spirit to rule the church (Acts 20:28), and in the First Letter of Peter they are exhorted to rule the flock of Christ in the manner of Christ the chief shepherd (1 Pt 5:1–4).

The New Testament does not provide all the information we would require to ascertain who presided at the liturgy, the church's most priestly activity. The Catholic tradition has generally assumed that the apostles designated bishops, presbyters, or their equivalents to perform this function. Perhaps in the very early stages, when the permanent structures of the church were still in the process of formation, persons without priestly ordination may have had the capacity to preside at the eucharist, but if so these practices are not normative for the church of later ages.

The evidence for the time of the Apostolic Fathers is still fragmentary and controverted. A very early work, the *Didache,* speaks of the prophets as "high priests" (13:3) and, probably referring to the eucharist, remarks that the prophets may give thanks as long as they wish (10:7). Some have inferred from this that the prophets in Syria were authorized to preside at the eucharist, but it is not evident that "giving thanks" is in this case identical with presiding at the eucharist, nor can we be certain that the prophets in question were not appointed to an office that would be, in later terminology, priestly. Ignatius of Antioch says in his Letter to the Smyrnians (8) that a eucharist is not valid unless celebrated by the bishop or someone whom he appoints. Some commentators such as Pierre Grelot infer that the delegation in question would be to a member of the presbyterium.[6]

In documents of the early third century, such as the *Apostolic Tradition* of Hippolytus, we see bishops as pastoral leaders and high priests of worship holding a clear primacy over other ministers. The ordination ritual for the presbyter given by Hippolytus speaks only of the presbyter's tasks in the government of the people of God. There is no indication that presbyters are expected either to preach or to celebrate the eucharist. The main function of the presbyter at this point would seem to have been the providing of advice and assistance to the *episkopos*. By the end of the fourth century, however, the presbyters had taken on a leadership role in the celebration of the liturgy and in preaching. During the Middle Ages the presbyters were increasingly seen as the normal presiders at the eucharist, and hence as having everything requisite for ministerial priesthood. Thomas Aquinas relates Christian priesthood primarily to the offering of the eucharist.

Vatican II on the Two Priesthoods

Official Catholic teaching on priesthood, as I have already mentioned, has undergone a recent shift, signalized by Vatican II. Article 10 of LG declares that there are in the church two essentially different types of priesthood, both of them participations in the priestly office of Christ. The first is the general or common priesthood of all the faithful. This common priesthood is acquired through being consecrated to God in baptism and is exercised first of all by witnessing to Christ (the prophetic function), secondly by joining in offering the eucharistic sacrifice, by prayer, thanksgiving, and the reception of the sacraments (priestly functions), and thirdly by the personal and social conduct of Christians in their secular life (royal functions).

This common priesthood belongs to the whole people of God, not simply to the laity. Lay persons share the common priesthood with clergy and religious. The role of the laity is spelled out in greater detail in chapter 4 of LG, articles 30–38, and still more fully in the Decree on the Apostolate of the Laity. In each of these texts a distinction is made between the prophetic, priestly, and royal offices of Christ, in all three of which the laity participate. Thus it is necessary to keep in mind that the common priesthood involves more than specifically priestly functions. The word "priestly" is used to designate two different things—participation in the mediatorial office of Christ as a whole and participation specifically in Christ's role of worship.

After discussing the common priesthood, LG 10 takes up the ministerial or hierarchical priesthood, which it describes predominantly in terms of its sacral functions: the sacred power that reaches its apex in the offering of the eucharistic sacrifice in the person of Christ and in the name of the whole people. But when the Constitution returns to a more detailed discussion of the presbyterate in article 28 it gives approximately equal weight to all three functions, declaring that presbyters "are consecrated to preach the gospel, shepherd the faithful, and celebrate divine worship as true priests of the New Testament."

Some commentators have had difficulty about the statement of LG 10 that the two kinds of priesthood in the church differ not only in degree but in essence, but the statement is clear and helpful so far as it goes. It obviously does not mean that the ordained priest undergoes an essential change, thereby ceasing to be a partaker in our common humanity. The distinction is not between two kinds of person but two kinds of priesthood. The council refuses to attribute a higher grade or degree to the ministerial, as though the common priesthood ranked lower than it on the same scale. Instead, it situates the two kinds of priesthood in different categories, like oranges and apples. The ministerial priesthood involves a public representational function rather than a personal giftedness. If anything, the common priesthood is more exalted, for the ministers are ordained for the sake of service toward the whole people of God.

The Priestly Character

Following medieval tradition, the Council of Trent taught that an indelible character is imprinted by three sacraments: baptism, confirmation, and ordination. According to Thomas Aquinas, each of these sacraments imprints a particular configuration to Christ the eternal priest in matters that pertain to divine worship.[7] The idea of an indelible character, properly understood, contributes to our understanding of priestly ordination. It implies that this sacrament can never be repeated. Even if a person withdraws from the active ministry, the character remains. Because of its permanent nature, the character calls for a total and lasting commitment. It grasps the whole being of the person ordained, so that he becomes a man of God, not simply a delegate of the community. The principal agent in ordaining is not the community or even the bishop or bishops; it is Christ the Lord, who confers a share in his own eternal priesthood. As Yves Congar understands it, ordination is "an act of the risen Christ mediated through the already existing office, which is itself in historical continuity with the apostolic community."[8] Because the risen Christ is active in ordination, so is the Holy Spirit. According to Acts 20:26, the presbyter-bishops of Ephesus have been commissioned by the Holy Spirit to feed and guard the flock of Christ.

As I have indicated, there is some debate among contemporary authors about whether the priestly character is ontological or merely functional. In accordance with authoritative teaching on the nature of episcopal consecration, it seems that the character imparted must be in some sense ontological: it is a consecration affecting the new priest in his very being.[9] But the character is also functional in the sense that it is dynamic; it imparts a radical capacity and aptitude to perform certain acts. Metaphysically, I suppose, the character could be described as a spiritual quality, and more technically as a *habitus,* belonging to the supernatural order.[10]

Ordination imparts a new relationship not only to Christ the head but also to other members of the body of Christ. In particular, it makes one a member of the order of presbyters, who together with the bishops and in subordination to them have responsibility for the communal life of the whole church. In most cases the presbyter also enters into a particular presbyterium, either diocesan or religious, which is corporately committed to pastoral ministry with and under the diocesan bishop.

Office and Charism

The study of priesthood raises in acute form the question concerning the relationship between office and charism. It is quite proper to speak of charisms of priestly ministry, since the Holy Spirit is involved in the call and is given for the exercise of the office. But the charism does not by itself suffice to constitute priesthood. The vocation must be recognized publicly in the church and sealed sacramentally through ordination. The sacrament of ordination normally intensifies the charismatic gifts, as may be inferred from various statements in the two canonical Letters to Timothy (1 Tim 4:14 and 2 Tim 1:6). The charism, according to the Second Letter to Timothy, must be stirred up and rekindled through personal piety. In my final chapter, dealing with priestly spirituality, I shall return to this point. For present purposes, it may suffice to note that those who are ordained receive permanently the powers essentially pertaining to the priesthood, even if they fail to live up to the charism. Thus, office and charism are to some degree separable.

In connection with priestly office the question is sometimes asked whether ordination is absolute or relative. It is always relative, I would say, in the sense that it is for the sake of service toward the people of God. But it is absolute in the sense of not being restricted to a particular diocese or pastoral assignment. It imparts a general aptitude for public ministry in a variety of pastoral assignments and in any diocese. For the exercise of these pastoral powers, however, the priest must receive a canonical mission, which normally comes from the bishop according to canon law.

Representative Role of the Priest

In an effort to clarify the nature of presbyterate, many theologians use the category of representation. The ministerial priest, they say, is a public representative of the church and, on occasion, of Christ as Lord of the church. The term "representative" calls for some clarification, since it is frequently used to mean a mere substitution of one person for others. In theology, however, the idea of representation is not juridical but organic. The priest is configured to Christ in order that Christ may act in him as an instrument. The church, as Christ's mystical body, uses its priests not to pray or worship in its place but to be the organs through which it prays and professes its faith.[11] The acts of the church and of Christ as its head cannot be performed except by those who are publicly and sacramentally qualified through ordination. These acts, pertaining intimately to the order of salvation, cannot be done vicariously, by someone who has merely delegated power.

Archbishop Daniel Pilarczyk at the Synod of Bishops in 1990 proposed a concise definition, which felicitously gathers up many of the same ideas that I have sought to propose in this paper. He wrote: "The priest [i.e., presbyter] is a member of the Christian faithful who has been permanently configured by Christ through holy orders to serve the Church, in collaboration with the local bishop, as representative and agent of Christ, the head of the Church, and therefore as representative and agent of the Church community before God and the world."[12]

By the "permanent configuration" in this definition, Archbishop Pilarczyk evidently means the so-called indelible character. In accordance with Vatican II, the archbishop gives a somewhat broader interpretation to the "character" than did Thomas Aquinas, relating it not simply to worship but to all three of the presbyter's functions.

Archbishop Pilarczyk's definition is valuable for the emphasis it places on the christological and ecclesial dimensions of priesthood. I would say, in agreement with him, that the priest is, by ordination, an ecclesiastical person, one who embodies in a public way the existence of the church itself. More than this, the priest is an agent and representative of Christ himself. In order that the church may be effectively subject to Christ as its living

Lord, it is necessary that there be persons and actions wherein Christ makes himself visibly and sacramentally present.

No sharp distinction can be made between the activities of Christ and of the church. Because the church remains at the service of Christ, who must act visibly through his representatives, the priest must have, on occasion, a capacity to act in the person of Christ as head of the church. Such activity may fall into the categories of teaching, worship, or pastoral rule, but is not reducible to any one of them alone. When the priest acts as a pure instrument, he is not using his own power but simply allowing the power of Christ or the Holy Spirit to work through him. Talk about the "sacred powers" of the priesthood can therefore be misleading.

There is nothing to prevent the laity from being used for certain functions by Christ or the church as instruments, but when this happens they do not act by virtue of a sacramental character that gives them a public status in the church. The priest alone is the minister radically empowered to be a public representative of the church and of Christ when he acts as Lord of the church. This concept of priesthood applies primarily to the bishop, who has the fullness of priesthood, but it applies also to the presbyter who participates in a lesser degree in that same priesthood.

II. THE MINISTRY OF THE WORD

THE COUNCIL OF TRENT, as we have seen, defined priesthood in terms of cultic action, putting the emphasis on sacraments and sacramental sacrifice rather than on the ministry of the word. But the same council drew up a reform decree on instruction and preaching in which it sternly admonished bishops that the preaching of the gospel was their chief task *(praecipuum episcoporum munus)*. This decree also mentioned priests as persons whom the bishop might suitably appoint to nourish the people committed to their charge with the words of salvation.[1]

Vatican II

Following the indications of this text, Vatican II in LG 25 declared that preaching was the preeminent task of bishops, who were to be heralds of the faith, bringing new disciples to Christ, and authentic teachers endowed with the authority of Christ to preach to the people entrusted to their care. Only after discussing the bishop's ministry of the word did Vatican II go on in subsequent paragraphs to explain their ministry of the sacraments and of pastoral government (LG 26 and 27).

When it turns to the three functions of the presbyter in LG 28, the council states simply that they are consecrated to preach the gospel, shepherd the faithful, and celebrate divine worship as true priests *(sacerdotes)* of the New Testament. The text gives no special priority to the ministry of the word. A more detailed treatment of the presbyteral office may be found in the Decree on the Ministry and Life of Priests, which in its second chapter surveys the functions of priests under the three headings of the prophetic, the priestly, and the pastoral. In this text the council seems to give a certain priority to the ministry of the word. Presbyters, it declares, as fellow-workers of bishops, have as their first charge to announce the gospel of God to all in order to establish and build up the people of God (PO 4). In this way they carry out the command of the Lord to "Go into the whole world and preach the gospel to every creature" (Mk 16:15). The council in this connection points out that faith, which is necessary for salvation, comes from hearing the preaching of Christ, as Paul teaches in Romans 10:17.

PO 2 emphasizes the close bonds between the bishop and the presbyters in the service of the gospel—a term that surely implies preaching and teaching. Certain men, it declares, were "installed in the order of the presbyterate in order to be collaborators with the episcopal order in carrying out the apostolic mission entrusted to them by Christ." The Decree on the Pastoral Office of Bishops speaks of parish priests *(parochi)* as having a teaching office *(munus docendi)* in their role as cooperators with the bishop (CD 30).

Among the responsibilities of presbyters underlined by Vatican II, the preaching of homilies holds an important place. The Decree on the Ministry and Life of Priests emphasizes that in their preaching priests should be conscious of their responsibility "not to teach their own wisdom but God's Word" (PO 4). "They should not expound the word of God in merely general and abstract terms, but must apply the perennial truth of the gospel to the concrete circumstances of life" (ibid.). The Constitution on the Liturgy says that the homily forms part of the liturgy itself, and is not to be omitted on Sundays and feast days except for grave reasons. Through the homily, says the council, "the mysteries of the faith and the norms of Christian life are to be explained on the basis of the sacred texts" (SC 52). The Constitution on

Divine Revelation, in its final chapter on the Bible in the life of the church, encourages priests to study the sacred page in order to nourish the people of God with the food of the scriptures, so as by this means to enlighten their minds, strengthen their wills, and fire their hearts with the love of God (DV 23–25).

At this point I should like to turn to the work of contemporary theologians. Three of the most prominent German-speaking theologians—Karl Rahner, Hans Urs von Balthasar, and Joseph Ratzinger—have placed special emphasis on the prophetic function in their theology of priesthood.

Rahner

Karl Rahner sets out from the idea that the word of God is a salutary word that brings about that which it proclaims. God's word reaches its culmination in the incarnation, in which the Word becomes flesh for the sake of our redemption. In the church the prophetic no longer looks forward to some saving act that is still to come, but it makes present the reality that has already been given in Jesus Christ. The word of Christian proclamation, when spoken with prophetic power, brings about the saving presence of Christ and leads to faith and conversion.

Any Christian can bear witness to his or her own faith, but the priest is empowered from above to bear witness immediately to Christ. "The priest," says Rahner, "is he to whom the efficacious word of God has been entrusted."[2] The priest does not speak of or for himself, but only as an emissary, a herald, a messenger. The word that he speaks as priest is not just a word about God, such as the theologian might utter. The priest as witness finds himself possessed by the word of which he is the bearer. The word, spoken rightly, wants to absorb the whole life of the priest and subject it to itself.[3] Rahner can therefore propose the following definition of the ministerial priest:

The priest is the proclaimer of the word of God, officially commissioned and appointed as such by the Church as a whole in such a way that this word is entrusted to him in the supreme degree of sacramental intensity present in it. His work as proclaimer of the word is in this sense essentially directed towards the community (which is at least potentially in existence). To express the matter quite simply, he is the one sent by the Church to proclaim the gospel in her name.[4]

Rahner's theology of priesthood is bound up with his understanding of the word of God as a salutary word that actually accomplishes what it affirms.[5] "The word of preaching," he declares, "is the efficacious proclamation which brings about what it speaks of, the grace announced: it is truly the word of life, creative word of God."[6]

To some degree God is always present in his word, but this occurs with varying degrees of concentration and intensity. The supreme realization of the efficacious word of God occurs in the sacraments. In the eucharist the word comes to an unsurpassable climax, for in this sacrament the incarnate Logos of God becomes truly and substantially present. In it the death and resurrection of the Lord and his future coming are exhibited and proclaimed.[7]

From this point of view we can understand why ministry in the New Testament is described predominantly with reference to the word rather than to the sacraments. Rahner, wishing to preserve both aspects, does so by including the sacramental and cultic dimension under the ministry of the word. What about the third function, that of pastoral government? Rahner seems to subsume that task likewise under the rubric of proclamation, insofar as the community is brought about and sustained by the hearing of God's word. Many leadership functions in the church, he remarks, may be conferred upon members of the faithful who are not priests.[8] In the writings of his that I have seen, Rahner is rather vague on the pastoral responsibilities proper to the presbyter. Perhaps that is because as a religious priest he was generally free from parochial duties.

Balthasar

Not unlike Rahner's approach is that of Hans Urs von Balthasar. In a recently translated article on "The Priest of the New Covenant" he takes his departure from Christology and more specifically from the mission of Jesus to proclaim the gospel.[9] Among the many passages he quotes from the Fourth Gospel is the following statement of Jesus: "I do not speak of my own accord but the Father who sent me commanded me what to say and how to say it" (Jn 12:47). The same idea of sending and obedience is brought out in another of his favorite Johannine passages, in which Jesus is quoted as saying: "The word that you hear is not mine but the Father's who sent me" (Jn 14:24).

Moving on to the ministry of the apostles, Balthasar declares that their mission from Jesus parallels that of Jesus from the Father. This biblical theme of representation is found in the saying of Jesus to the apostles, "As the Father has sent me, so I send you" (Jn 20:21). It is also found in the saying quoted by Luke with reference to the mission of the seventy disciples: "Whoever hears you hears me" (Lk 10:16). The disciples are sent out first of all to proclaim the good news and in that connection to do the deeds of Jesus Christ.

Turning then to the apostolic age, Balthasar emphasizes Paul's consciousness of being sent to proclaim the gospel (1 Cor 1:17). Writing to the Thessalonians, Paul gives thanks "that when you received the word of God which you heard from us, you accepted it not as the word of men but as what it really is, the word of God, which is at work in you believers" (1 Thess 2:13). Conscious of being a fellow-worker of God, Paul describes his proclamation of the gospel as a "priestly service" (Rom 15:16). But the ministry of the word flows over into deed. The celebration of the Lord's

Supper is the high point of proclamation, for in it the death of the Lord is proclaimed (1 Cor 11:26).

In the second half of his essay on priesthood, Balthasar supplements these ideas on the ministry of the word by reference to the biblical imagery of the shepherd. Jesus the chief shepherd not only calls the sheep, but also loves them, guards them, and lays down his life for them. Relying on this imagery, Balthasar can maintain that priestly ministry in the New Testament involves tireless commitment to service and self-sacrifice for the sake of the flock. Whether one takes proclamation or shepherding as the key concept, in either case a certain "over-againstness" must be recognized. Speaking with authority, the herald or the shepherd stands "over against" the hearers and followers. The apostolic word of preaching therefore includes the authority to call for obedience and assent, and the power of binding and loosing in the community. Like Rahner, therefore, Balthasar sees the ministries of sacramental worship and pastoral government as implied in, and deriving from, the authoritative ministry of the word.

Ratzinger

As a third and final representative of the word-centered concept of priesthood I should like to instance Joseph Ratzinger, especially in his early work. In 1959, several years before the council, he published *The Open Circle,* a small book in which he emphasized the fundamental equality of all Christians.[10] Protesting against an exaggerated separation between the special ministry of the ordained and the general priesthood of the faithful, he indicated a distaste for sacerdotal and hierarchical language.

At the time of Vatican II, Ratzinger expressed his enthusiasm for the Decree on the Ministry and Life of Priests, which in his view overcame the excessive emphasis on priesthood and sacrifice in medieval theology, and took seriously the challenges of Luther to return to an authentic New Testament understanding of ministry.[11]

PO, he observed, "has now eliminated the one-sided emphasis on the idea of priesthood as sacrifice." He quoted with satisfaction the statement in PO 4: "It is the first duty of the priest to proclaim the gospel of God to all." Ratzinger recognized, however, that in placing the accent on the ministry of the word, the council did not neglect the other essentials of the ministerial office. Presiding over the eucharist, the priest makes present the redemptive reality itself and gathers the community around the table of the Lord.[12]

In several articles published in the late 1960s Ratzinger continued to emphasize the primacy of the word in priestly ministry.[13] In relationship to the functions of worship and pastoral government, he maintained, the prophetic office is more fundamental and more encompassing. The priest is not primarily a cultic figure but an evangelist. This priority of the word, however, does not displace the sacramental or pastoral dimensions. Word and sacrament are inseparable. The eucharist itself, as a powerful form of the word, fulfills the gospel by rendering the paschal mystery present. Pastoral office must be understood as service of the word, modeled on the figure of Christ the good Shepherd.

In his more recent writings Ratzinger speaks increasingly of the authority of the priest as representing Christ the Lord. Ordained in the apostolic succession, the priest shares in the apostolic ministry of the bishop. "The apostle," he writes, "acts not out of his own authority but Christ's, not as a member of the community, but as over against the community and addressing it in Christ's name."[14] Since the word of God always comes from above, and transmits itself in history, the church necessarily has a dialogic structure. The church therefore requires an official ministry that stands with Christ and represents him to the community. Bishops and presbyters are ordained to persevere in the teaching of the apostles.

Having looked at the work of three prominent theologians, I should like to turn now to Popes Paul VI and John Paul II, especially to examine what they say about priesthood in relation to evangelization.

Paul VI

An important shift in Catholic ecclesiology since Vatican II has been the new emphasis on evangelization. Paul VI, a decade after the close of the council, summed up the objectives of the council under one single rubric: "to make the Church of the twentieth century ever better fitted for proclaiming the gospel to the people of the twentieth century."[15] By this accent of contemporaneity, the pope links himself with Vatican II's program of *aggiornamento*. But at the same time, his emphasis is thoroughly biblical and traditional. He founds the whole program christologically, by a description of Jesus Christ as the first and greatest evangelizer. Jesus began his ministry with the announcement "I must proclaim the good news of the Kingdom of God. This is what I was sent to do" (Lk 4:43; EN 6).

Evangelizing—the pope goes on to say—is the grace and vocation proper to the church, its deepest identity. It exists in order to evangelize, which means in the first place to preach and to teach, to proclaim with authority the word of God, though evangelization is also carried on by means of sacramental and pastoral activities, all of which have as their goal to bring the gospel more effectively into the lives of individuals and communities (EN 14).

Primarily and immediately, said the pope, the mandate of Christ to preach the gospel to every creature pertains to the bishops with and under Peter (EN 67, quoting AG 38). Priests, he then added, are associated with bishops in the ministry of evangelization and are by a special title responsible for that task. He described the work of evangelization in very broad terms, namely: "to proclaim with authority the word of God, to assemble the scattered People of God, to feed this People with the signs of the action of Christ which are the sacraments, to set this People on the road to salvation, to maintain it in that unity of which we are, at different levels, active and living instruments, and unceasingly to keep this community gathered around Christ, faithful to its deepest vocation" (EN 68).

In the course of this exhortation Paul VI placed special emphasis on the ministry of the word. Serious preparation, he declares, is necessary for all who devote themselves to this ministry. "Being animated by the conviction, ceaselessly deepened, of the greatness and riches of the word of God, those who have the mission of transmitting it must give maximum attention to the dignity, precision, and adaptation of their language. Everyone knows that the art of speaking takes on today a very great importance. How would preachers and catechists be able to neglect this?" (EN 73).

In the same document Paul VI exhorted all evangelizers to "pray without ceasing to the Holy Spirit, the principal agent of evangelization, to guide them as the decisive inspirer of their plans, their initiatives, and their evangelizing activity" (EN 75). The pastoral service of the word requires courage and fidelity in preserving, defending, and communicating the truth of the gospel regardless of the sacrifices this involves. The God of truth, he writes, "expects us [priests] to be vigilant defenders and devoted preachers of the truth" (EN 78).

Among the many new accents in *Evangelii nuntiandi* we might dwell for a moment on the phrase, "the evangelization of cultures," which I suspect may have been an original coinage of the pope. He pointed out that, although the gospel can never be identified with culture, cultures can be more or less compatible with the gospel. The gospel is capable of regenerating and permeating a culture without becoming subject to it. The culture is important, because the church, in order to evangelize, must borrow elements from the culture. A particular problem of our day, though not of our day alone, is the split between the gospel and culture. That split makes it difficult for the church to proclaim its message and for people to hear and accept what the church has to proclaim.

John Paul II

Pope John Paul II follows closely in the footsteps of Vatican II and Paul VI. His teaching on the priestly ministry of the word is compactly summarized in the apostolic constitution on priestly formation, *Pastores dabo vobis* (1992), §26. The pope begins by recapitulating the teaching of Vatican II that the priest is, first of all, a minister of the word of God. This ministry involves calling every person to the obedience of faith and leading believers to an ever greater familiarity with the mystery of God, revealed and communicated to us in Christ. In order to perform this service, the priest must have intimate personal knowledge of the word of God. He should know the scripture not only in its exegetical and linguistic aspects but also in such a way that he puts on the mind of Christ, letting the word of God penetrate his thoughts and feelings, so that he becomes first of all a believer in the message he is to transmit to others. The priest, like any other believer, needs to be evangelized.

In proclaiming the word, the priest must be conscious that his words, like those of Christ, are not his own but those of the One who has sent him. He proclaims the word in his capacity as a qualified minister—i.e., as a sharer in the prophetic authority of Christ and the church. In order to be sure of transmitting the gospel in its fullness, the priest must have a special sensitivity, love, and docility to the living tradition of the church and to the magisterium as the authoritative interpreter of the word of God.

Taking up Paul VI's concern for evangelization, John Paul II strongly emphasizes the missionary dimension of priestly ministry. In his encyclical on Missionary Activity, *Redemptoris missio,* he quotes from PO 10 the statement: "The spiritual gift that presbyters have received in ordination prepares them not for any narrow and limited mission, but for the most universal and all-embracing mission of salvation 'to the end of the earth.' For every priestly ministry shares in the universal scope of the mission that Christ entrusted to his apostles" (PO 10; quoted in RM 67). All priests, therefore, should have the mind and heart of missionaries, open to the needs of those living far away as well as those living close at hand. In the area in which they work, they are not simply to serve as pastors of the Catholic people, but should be concerned with the evangelization of those who do not belong to the flock of Christ. Religious priests who belong to missionary institutes, of course, have a special responsibility to look outward. Their total gift of themselves through the vows witnesses very effectively to gospel values and gives special power to their apostolate.

Missionary activity has been primarily defined in terms of specific territories. But the boundaries between Christian and non-Christian parts of the world are becoming more fluid. Even within traditionally Christian countries there are regions and segments of the population that are still in need of initial evangelization. Others who have been exposed to the gospel may have fallen away from the faith or lapsed into a merely nominal Christianity. Some traditionally Christian countries stand in dire need of re-evangelization.

In a most interesting section of **Redemptoris missio** the pope speaks of the missionary needs of the exploding cities where huge masses of humanity are gathered in virtual anonymity. He mentions young people who lack effective religious guidance, and refers to the tremendous spiritual needs of migrants and refugees, who have in many cases fled from situations of political oppression and inhuman misery (RM 36b).

At one point in his encyclical John Paul II recalls how Saint Paul journeyed to Athens, the cultural center of the Greco-Roman world, to proclaim the gospel at the Areopagus, where the most influential intellectuals were accustomed to gather. Today, says the pope, a new culture is emerging under the aegis of contemporary means of communication. If the gospel is to make contact with this culture, people of faith must be at home with new languages, new techniques, and a new psychology. At this point he recalls what Paul VI had said about the tragic split between the gospel and culture that seems to characterize our time (RM 36c).

In speaking of new Areopagi, John Paul II adverts to the new worlds of scientific research, economics, political science, and international relations. Ordinarily speaking, he says, it will be the task of the laity to permeate the sciences and professions with Christian values and thus to bridge the gap between faith and culture. But it is the task of priests to motivate these initiatives and to arouse a lively ecclesial consciousness in lay apostles.[16]

This directive role of the priest is emphasized in the present pope's apostolic exhortation on catechesis, *Catechesi tradendae* (1979). To provide suitable catechetical instruction is a responsibility of pastors in which they may call upon the assistance of lay and religious teachers, but must themselves assume responsibility. To all priests he says: "Whether you are in charge of a parish, or are chaplains to primary or secondary schools or universities, or have responsibility for pastoral activity at any level, or are leaders of large or small communities, especially youth groups, the Church expects you to neglect nothing with a view to a well-organized and well-oriented catechetical effort" (CT 64). In his Holy Thursday letter to priests of 1993, John Paul emphasized that the implementation of the new *Catechism of the Catholic Church* is entrusted above all to pastors.

Liturgical Preaching

Vatican II, in its Constitution on the Liturgy, emphasized the centrality of the homily as an integral part of the liturgy:

> By means of the homily the mysteries of the faith and the guiding principles of the Christian life are explained from the sacred text during the course of the liturgical year. The homily, therefore, is to be highly esteemed as part of the liturgy itself; in fact, at those

Masses which are celebrated on Sundays and holy days of obligation with the people present, it should not be omitted except for a
serious reason. (§52)

The Code of Canon Law gives further provisions concerning
the preaching of the word of God. Canon 528 imposes a strict
obligation on the pastor to see to it that the word of God is
announced and that the faithful are instructed in the truths of the
faith, especially through the homily, which is to be given at the
eucharist on Sundays and holy days of obligation. According to
canon 767 the celebrant is normally to give the homily within the
liturgy, but when he does not himself preach, the homily is
reserved to another priest or deacon.

There exists a vast literature on the subject of homiletics. In
1982 the United States Bishops' Committee on Priestly Life and
Ministry published a very helpful pamphlet, *Fulfilled in Your
Hearing: The Homily in the Sunday Assembly.* This booklet
reminds preachers that what the majority of the faithful require
from them is "simply to hear a person of faith speaking...to people about faith and life."[17] It recommends attentive listening to the
word of God in scripture and an awareness of the actual situation
of the people in the congregation. To make sure that the homily
meets the real concerns of the congregation, the Bishops'
Committee recommends that members of the congregation be
involved in a homily preparation group. Such a team can assist
the priest in reflecting on the liturgical readings in advance. It is
also advisable for the homilist to solicit feedback after the sermon, so that the quality of the preaching may be improved.

Although a priest or deacon is normally expected to be the
homilist, canon 766 states that lay preaching may be necessary or
useful in particular cases. Examples readily come to mind; for
example, when a parish is entrusted to a lay catechist or pastoral
associate, who has the responsibility of conducting a service of
the word in the absence of a priest. Even when a priest is the celebrant, it may be appropriate that a lay person do the preaching on

some special occasion or for some particular reason. This could happen, for instance, if the priest were not comfortable or effective in preaching at a children's mass, or if the priest lacked facility in the language of the congregation, as often happens in the case of foreign-born priests. In such cases the celebrant could suitably invite a lay person to preach at his mass. The Code of Canon Law, in its treatment of lay preaching, makes no distinction between nonordained men and nonordained women. Technically speaking, preaching by an unordained religious or lay person is not a homily, but it is nevertheless an instance of preaching. The possibility of having lay preachers by way of exception does not absolve the pastor of his serious responsibility to see to it that the word of God is rightly proclaimed.

Conclusion

The ministry of the word, we may conclude, holds a certain priority among the tasks of the priest because unless the faith is proclaimed and received, none of the other activities of the church makes any sense. The task of proclamation, however, is not reserved exclusively to the ordained. All believers should give testimony to the great works of God in Jesus Christ and be prepared to give an account of the hope that is in them (cf. 1 Pet 3:15). Bishops, presbyters, and deacons are ordained to preach and teach with an authority of office that is not given to others. The homily in the liturgy is reserved to them. But the presbyter should not imagine that the homily alone satisfies his obligation to the ministry of the word. He is commissioned to be a leader in the task of evangelizing those who do not yet believe and to instruct the faithful as a collaborator of the bishop in the maintenance of sound doctrine. The priest has special responsibility to see that the word of God is effectively proclaimed and that those who preach and teach present that word faithfully and accurately.

III. THE MINISTRY OF WORSHIP

IN MY SECOND CHAPTER I spoke of the priest as minister of the word, which is generally listed as the first of the three *munera,* the other two being the ministries of worship and pastoral governance. In this third chapter we get to the second *munus,* which is essential for understanding why bishops and presbyters are called priests *(hiereis, sacerdotes).* According to the general understanding, a priest is publicly commissioned to offer worship on behalf of a whole people, and thereby to gain God's benevolence and favor toward those on whose behalf he ministers. This concept of priesthood—common to Judaism, Christianity, and many other religions—is magnificently encapsulated in Hebrews, chapter 5:1–4, which states: "Every high priest chosen from among men is appointed to act on behalf of men in relation to God, to offer gifts and sacrifices for sins. He can deal gently with the ignorant and wayward, since he himself is beset with weakness. Because of this he is bound to offer sacrifice for his own sins as well as for those of the people. And one does not take the honor upon himself, but he is called by God, just as Aaron was." The same chapter goes on to apply this definition to Christ, the high priest par excellence, pointing out how he offered up prayers and supplications, with loud cries and tears; how "he learned obedience by the things he suffered, and being made perfect became the source of eternal salvation to all who obey him" (vv. 7–9).

Priesthood of Christ

In the broadest terms, the priestly action of Jesus is one of mediation between God and sinful humanity. His mediation has both a descending and an ascending moment. Human beings, alienated from God by sin, were incapable of performing acts that would placate God and reestablish friendship and communion. God, however, took the initiative through the incarnation. "God was in Christ, reconciling the world to himself" (2 Cor 5:19). Because this is true, every adequate Christology must begin, so to speak, from above. But, having taken on human flesh, Jesus identifies himself with sinful humanity and addresses the Father from below.

Because it was his mission to heal our nature by assuming it, Jesus took upon himself a frail and vulnerable body. "He took our infirmities and bore our diseases" (Mt 8:17, quoting Is 53:4). He submitted to poverty, hunger, thirst, fatigue, temptation, rejection, ridicule, unjust judgment, torture, and a painful death so that there would be no human sorrow or weakness with which he would be unable to sympathize (cf. Heb 4:15).

The public ministry of Jesus was brief and moved speedily to its climax. He felt constrained until he could accomplish his baptism to the full (Lk 12:50). In his sacrifice of the cross, his supreme priestly act, he was both priest and victim. By the shedding of his blood he ratified the covenant of the New Testament, just as Moses had ratified the Old Covenant by pouring out the blood of calves and goats (Heb 9:18–19). The sacrifice of the cross was then completed through the glorification of the victim by the Father to whom the offering was made. In heaven, seated at the right hand of the divine majesty, Jesus continues his priestly work by making intercession "for those who draw near to God through him" (Heb 7:25).

The priesthood of Jesus, like all priesthood, is social and public. As priest he is mediator of the new and definitive covenant.

His priestly work, therefore, consists in the gathering of a covenant people, which he forms and directs through his appointed disciples. At the Last Supper he instituted the ritual sacrifice that would become the reenactment of his own self-oblation. The church, as Christ's continuing presence here below, continues to celebrate his sacrifice and to carry on his work of worship and intercession.

Ministerial Priests

In the New Testament, as I mentioned in my first chapter, Christ alone is portrayed as the priest of the New Covenant. The apostles, the ministers of the word, and the pastoral leaders are not given sacred titles. But because the people of God was a priestly people, it was inevitable and entirely proper that those who acted on its behalf in relation to God, and on Christ's behalf in relation to the people, would come to be regarded as priestly figures. The ministry by which a priestly people performs its essential tasks cannot but be priestly.

By the second century the bishops were already being designated as *sacerdotes,* and later in the patristic period the presbyters, who shared some of the functions of the bishops and were ordained by them, came to be regarded as *sacerdotes secundi ordinis* (second-order priests). The dominant functions of bishops and presbyters, as seen by the later Fathers and the medieval doctors, were priestly: those of prayer, worship, and sacramental ministry. Thomas Aquinas, for instance, teaches that the principal task of priests is to consecrate the eucharist. Other sacraments such as baptism and penance pertain to them because they dispose people to receive the eucharist (ST 3.67.2).

The Council of Trent, reacting against Protestant contentions, anathematized the position that the priesthood of the New Testament consisted in the mere power to preach the gospel. It defined priesthood primarily in terms of the powers to forgive sins and to offer the holy sacrifice of the mass (Session 23, chap. 1; DS 1764). The same council stated that the sacrament of priestly orders was instituted at the Last Supper when Jesus uttered the words, "Do this in commemoration of me" (Session 22, can. 2; DS 1752; quoting Lk 22:19 and 1 Cor 11:24). Certainly this was at least one essential stage in the constitution of the ministerial priesthood, and the most important step for the ministry of worship.

Priority of the Sacerdotal Function

Vatican II did not clearly reject the view of Trent that the priesthood of bishops and presbyters is to be defined above all in terms of its sacred functions. For example, PO 2 begins its treatment of the presbyterate by asserting that Christ the Lord appointed some of the faithful as ministers "who would have the sacred power of order within the company of the faithful, to offer sacrifice and forgive sins, and who would publicly discharge their sacerdotal function for the people in the name of Christ." LG 28 describes presbyters as "true priests of the New Testament" and states that "it is above all in the eucharistic worship or synaxis that they exercise their sacred function."

John Paul II seems to give priority to the sacerdotal function of the ordained. In his 1980 Holy Thursday Letter, *Dominicae cenae,* he holds that "the Eucharist is the principal and central *raison d'être* of the sacrament of the priesthood, which effectively came into being at the moment of the institution of the Eucharist and together with it." In the same context he goes on to say that "the priest fulfills his principal mission and is manifested in all his fullness when he celebrates the Eucharist, and this manifestation is more complete when he himself allows the depth of that mystery to become visible, so that it alone shines forth in people's hearts and minds through his ministry. This is the supreme exercise of the 'kingly priesthood,' 'the source and summit of all Christian life.'"[1] Without contradicting Vatican II, John Paul II remains close to Thomas Aquinas and Trent.

Ordination

It is firm Catholic teaching, reasserted in any number of official documents since Trent, that the ministerial priesthood is transmitted through ordination. Although Jesus constituted the apostles as priestly ministers he did not, in the usual sense of the word, "ordain" them. Ordination is rather the means by which the priesthood, once brought into existence, is perpetuated by being conferred on new members, who are coopted into the ministerial body by a rite that is itself a sacrament. According to the current practice, it takes place by the laying on of hands by the ordaining prelate together with the prayer for the grace of the Holy Spirit. In its primary significance, apostolic succession does not mean a historical replacement of the dead by the living, though the term might seem to suggest this. Rather, it signifies aggregation into the presently existing and living apostolic body.

The Council of Trent defined under anathema that the sacrament of ordination is the function of bishops (Session 23, can. 7, DS 1777). In the same canon it anathematized the view that the consent of the people was constitutive of the validity of sacramental ordination. Vatican II, in similar fashion, spoke of the bishops as "dispensers of sacred orders" (LG 26). But it by no means ruled out the idea that the lay members of the church should be able to signify their consent, in accordance with the principle that the church should be an organic or ordered whole under the direction of the bishops (SC 26).

Luther, in the first period after his break from Rome, spoke vehemently against the Catholic doctrine of ordination and sought to reduce priesthood to the ministry of the word. The sacrament of holy orders, he wrote, "can be no more than a rite by which to choose a speaker in the Church." With this purely functional interpretation of office he felt authorized to declare: "He [the priest] is distinguished from the layman only by what he does." In his tract on ***The Babylonian Captivity of the Church*** he wrote concerning the sacrament of ordination: "The Church of Christ does not know this sacrament; it was invented by the pope's Church."[2]

It would be pointless to mention these polemical statements of the early Luther except that certain contemporary Catholics are moving in much the same direction. Following Küng and Schillebeeckx, whose views have been discussed in my first chapter, Leonardo Boff has urged that in the absence of an ordained minister, a basic community can truly celebrate the Lord's Supper in which Christ is truly, and in some degree sacramentally, present.[3] This view, like those of Küng and Schillebeeckx, has been rejected by the CDF.[4] The point at issue is that the sacraments are public acts of the church as such, and cannot be celebrated by an individual or a particular congregation except in union with the bishop and the body of bishops. Only through ordinations conferred by the apostolic body can individuals enter into the public ministry. The deviant views would make sense only in terms of a congregational ecclesiology that is far from Catholic.[5] The ordained are not mere delegates of the assembly to which they minister. They receive their gifts through apostolic succession in office, which confers upon them the sacred character of order, empowering them to act in the name of the church and in the name of Christ as head of the church. This double empowerment, which comes to clearest expression in worship, may here be analyzed in greater detail.

The Ecclesial Dimension

All the sacraments are sacraments of the church. It is not just the individual priest who baptizes, who forgives sins, who offers the eucharistic sacrifice, and dispenses the other sacraments. The priest does so on behalf of the church and as its authorized agent. "Agent" in this context does not mean "substitute." The priest does not act in place of the church, but the church acts in and through him as its representative.

No human group can constitute itself as a church; it becomes a church by being received as such by the universal church. In this light we can see why the priest is not installed in office by the local community. He is the representative of the bishop, who in turn is the bond of union between the particular church and the universal church.[6] Even if bishops or priests are chosen by some electoral process, they have to receive the laying on of hands by previously ordained bishops.

Just as the priest conducts sacramental worship in the name of the church, so too in the creed he professes the faith of the church, of which he is an officially ordained bearer. The priest is also charged to offer prayer in the name of the church. This is especially true of liturgical prayer, which enters into the ministry of the sacraments and the canonical hours. Although the liturgy of the hours is the prayer of the whole church, the priest is charged by his office to lead the people in this prayer, through which Christ continues his prayer in his body, the church.

The Christological Dimension

It is not enough, however, to see the priest as minister of the church; he is also ordained to be minister of Christ. In every sacrament Christ is the principal agent. The priest or celebrant can be no more than an instrumental cause. As Augustine put it, when Peter or Judas baptizes, Christ baptizes.

Certain sacraments, as is well known, are reserved to the priest who publicly represents the church. Although anyone can validly baptize and may licitly do so in case of an emergency, five of the sacraments—namely confirmation, ordination, penance, the eucharist, and the anointing of the sick—are reserved to priests (presbyters or bishops, as the case may be). In his ministry, the priest does not exercise his own powers, but acts instrumentally, in virtue of the power of Christ, who makes himself actively present through the Holy Spirit.

In much of the contemporary literature it has become common to speak of the priest as "presider." Up to a point, this usage is correct, for the priest does have the responsibility to regulate and coordinate the liturgical celebration. But he does more than regulate the service, more than perform the prophetic function of preaching the word of God. In administering the sacraments the celebrant exercises a properly sacred ministry, participating in the priestly power of Christ, as the sacrament of ordination has made him capable of doing.

Many documents of the magisterium, following Thomas Aquinas and other masters, speak of the priest acting in the person of the church and in the person of Christ.[7] These terms are not always used with exactly the same meaning, but the general sense may here be indicated.

In any sacramental action the priest acts by the power of Christ and in the name of Christ. When the priest is said to act "in the person of Christ," emphasis is placed on the specifically divine quality of the effect that is produced thanks to the principal causality of Christ as head of the church. In this capacity the priest is set "over against" the rest of the body of Christ. St. Thomas says, for example, that a bishop can dispense a person from a vow made to God because Christ, who is God, acts in the person of the bishop.[8]

Penance

The expression *in persona Christi* fits well into the context of divine forgiveness, inasmuch as it originated in the Vulgate translation of 2 Corinthians 2:10, where Paul says that he pardons the community "in the person of Christ."[9] In his apostolic exhortation on ***Reconciliation and Penance*** (1984), John Paul II points out that the priest acts in the sacrament of penance in the person of Christ, in whose name he absolves the sinner.[10] The present pope displays a special affection for this sacrament, which he calls "the tribunal of mercy rather than of strict and rigorous justice" (R&P 31). Of all priestly ministries, he says, "this is undoubtedly the most difficult and sensitive, the most exhausting and demanding, ... but also one of the most beautiful and consoling" (R&P 29). Ordinarily, he holds, penance should be administered after individual confession, in which the dialogue between the penitent and the confessor provides for suitable advice and salutary reparation (R&P 32). While the pope clearly favors auricular confession, he makes provision for the conduct of communal penance services and even for general absolution in circumstances where individual confession would not be practical or possible. He adds the reminder, however, that "there remains unchanged the obligation to make an individual confession of serious sins before again having recourse to another general absolution" (R&P 33).

One of the forgotten truths revived at Vatican II was the ecclesial dimension of the sacraments in general, and of penance in particular. According to the plan of God a double reconciliation takes place. The sinner is restored to full communion with the church—a communion impaired by sin—and thereby brought into a new relationship with God. Pope John Paul II, taking up this theme, calls attention to the social nature of the sacrament of penance, in which, he says, "the whole Church comes to the aid of the penitent and welcomes him again into her bosom, especially as it was the whole Church that was wounded by his sin. As the minister of penance, the priest by virtue of his sacred office appears as the witness and representative of this ecclesial nature of the sacrament" (R&P 31, iv).

Eucharist

The term *in persona Christi* is most frequently used in connection with the words of consecration uttered by the priest at the eucharist. Here, as in the case of penance, it is important to keep in mind both the ecclesial and the christological aspects. Robert Sokolowski has carefully analyzed these two dimensions in his book *Eucharistic Presence*.[11] Most of the prayers said by the priest during the mass are expressed in the first person plural. The priest says that we come before God confessing our sins, asking for forgiveness, praising and thanking God, and imploring God's blessing. After a brief invocation of the Holy Spirit the celebrant goes into the narrative describing the Last Supper, and at a central point of that narrative he breaks into the very words of Jesus, uttering them in the first person singular. He also shifts into the present tense, saying, "Take and eat, this is my body...." The effect is entirely different than it would be if the priest kept to the past tense and indirect discourse, informing the congregation that Jesus had told the apostles that they should take and eat. The past tense and indirect statement would prevent the efficacious significance of the words from coming to expression. Sokolowski even asserts that otherwise "What happened at the Last Supper would not be permitted to happen again" (p. 84). Speaking as he does in the very person of the living Christ, the priest allows Christ to speak in him, making Christ's own sacrifice present in a new way. Pius XII in his encyclical on the liturgy, *Mediator Dei,* quotes from John Chrysostom the statement that the priest "lends his tongue, gives his hand" to Christ.[12]

For our purposes today it is important to add that the words do not effect the sacrifice except when spoken by someone capable of speaking and acting in the person of Christ the head of the church. No one can take it upon himself to perform this function. Sacramental ordination to priestly office confers the power to pronounce the words of consecration in such a way that Christ is the principal speaker and actor.[13] Only in this way is it possible for the eucharist to be identically the same sacrifice that was offered on Calvary. As the Council of Trent clearly taught, the priest and the victim are the same; only the manner of offering is different.[14]

Very valuable for the priest, in my opinion, is Monsignor Sokolowski's distinction between sacramental quotation and dramatic presentation. The priest at the altar is not supposed to attempt a vivid depiction or imitation of the action of Christ, or to embellish Christ's words through dramatization. Such behavior can actually distract the congregation from the true meaning and content of the sacrifice. The words quoted by the priest "presuppose an emptying of the performative self before the power and efficacy of the divine Word." The less the congregation are distracted by the priest's personal style, the more likely they are to observe that the self-effacement of Christ himself serves as a model for the priest's *persona*.[15]

While emphasizing the unique role of the priest at the eucharist, we ought not to imagine that the congregation consists of merely passive spectators or recipients. Long before Vatican II, Pius XII in his encyclical ***Mediator Dei*** on the sacred liturgy (1947) insisted on the active participation of the laity, declaring that they offer the sacrifice through the hands of the priest. In the Roman canon, the pope observed, the priest refers to the eucharist as "my sacrifice and yours."[16] By virtue of their baptism, the faithful have received an indelible character that makes them participants in the priesthood of Christ and equips them to offer liturgical worship to God. At the eucharist they offer the sacrifice by the hands of the ministerial priest and in union with him. When they receive communion they in some way complete the sacrifice in the offering of which they have already taken part. No dichotomy should be made between the sacrifice and the banquet; both are essential to the one action that is a sacrificial banquet.

Vatican II followed essentially the teaching of Pius XII on this point. In LG 10 it taught that the ministerial priest, acting in the person of Christ, brings about the eucharistic sacrifice and offers this to God in the name of the whole people. Again in LG 17 it declared that although all the faithful can baptize, the priest alone can complete the building up of the Body in the eucharistic sacrifice. In SC 48 the people are exhorted to offer the immaculate victim together with the priest, who acts in the person of Christ. Thus the documents of Vatican II, while insisting that the priest and laity act together in the offering of the sacrifice, make it clear that they have essentially different roles. No room is left for the opinion that the priest is a mere deputy of the congregation or that the congregation can offer a true eucharist without an ordained priest.

Ordination of Women

The fact that the priest in the eucharist acts in the person of Christ is of some importance in connection with an issue much discussed in our day, the ordination of women. Relying on certain texts from Bonaventure, Thomas Aquinas, and others, the CDF Declaration on the Admission of Women to the Ministerial Priesthood, *Inter Insigniores* (1976), maintained that in order to act in the person of Christ the priest must bear a certain natural resemblance to Christ and be his very image. The maleness of Christ is in this case not a mere accident, like his having a beard or brown eyes. It belongs to the very nature of his role, which corresponds to that of Yahweh as husband of Israel. Christ at the eucharist acts as head and bridegroom of the church, which is both his body and his bride. He offers the sacrifice by which he sanctifies his beloved bride, in order to make her holy and without blemish (cf. Eph 5:25–27).

This argument does not by itself prove that Christ could not have called women to the ministerial priesthood, but it offers a theological reason that makes it intelligible why he would not have done so. The New Testament presents Jesus as having called only men to apostolic mission and commanded only men to celebrate the memorial meal of the Lord's Supper. In accordance with that precedent, the early church selected only men for episcopal or presbyteral office, although women played other roles of great importance in the apostolic communities. The tradition of the Catholic Church throughout the centuries has been steadfast on this point. Whenever the question of a female priesthood has arisen, as has in fact happened at various points in history, Catholic bishops and theologians have given a unanimously negative response. For this reason Pope Paul VI, followed by John Paul II, has done the same. John Paul II has made it clear that the question is not dogmatically open; it has been definitively settled. Any doubt about this matter should be removed by the response of the Congregation to the *Dubium* issued with the approval of the pope on October 28, 1995. Ratzinger here stated that the teaching of the pope on this point is infallible by reason of the consensus on which it rests; it is supported by the ordinary universal magisterium of the bishops in the past and in the present.

Popular Piety

Passing to another and a final question, one may ask how the church's life of worship can be rendered more intense and lively. Many liturgical scholars are concerned that the devotional life of the faithful seems to have declined in spite of, or perhaps because of, the reforms of Vatican II. The council made an effort to center the life of worship more on scripture and on the sacraments, especially on the eucharist as the chief sacrament. But in implementing the council, the liturgical reformers unwittingly destroyed many forms of piety that had sustained the devotion of the faithful in recent centuries. In countries such as our own there is a paucity of popular devotions, although in some circles there has been a flowering of devotions based on dubious and unapproved apparitions. The charismatic renewal for a time filled in the void, but it seems to have lost some of its vitality in recent years. It would seem to be a major responsibility of priests to foster forms of devotion that are sound, traditional, and at the same time popular.

Dr. Eamon Duffy, of the University of Cambridge, has recently argued that the liturgical movement that triumphed at Vatican II suffered from certain blind spots. "Too much attention was paid to text and rubric in liturgical rites, too little to the concrete embedding of liturgy in social reality, and the complex uses to which the Christian people actually put the language of liturgy and sacrament. In the process, liturgical theorists gave too little value to the paraliturgical proliferation of secondary rites, and what they thought of as the clutter of sacramentals[,] which ... was a sign not of decadence but of vigorous lay appropriation of the meaning of the liturgy."[17]

Among such popular devotions, some are closely connected with the eucharist itself. The pope in his Holy Thursday letter **Dominicae cenae** (1980) taught that eucharistic worship should not be restricted to the time of mass. He recommended personal prayer before the Blessed Sacrament, hours of adoration, periods of exposition, eucharistic benediction, and eucharistic congresses. Such practices are not contrary to the letter or the spirit of Vatican II. As the pope put it, "All this therefore corresponds to the general principles and particular norms already long in existence but newly formulated during and after the Second Vatican Council."[18] In many parishes these practices, which some regarded as outmoded since Vatican II, have been making a recovery. It is not a question of reversing the reforms of Vatican II, but of implementing them in ways that take better account of the dynamics of faith and worship.

Conclusion

In reaction against medieval sacralism, Catholic theology since Vatican II has tended to deemphasize the hieratic or sacerdotal aspect of priestly ministry. This shift, in my opinion, has been partly responsible for the crisis of priestly identity and for the paucity of vocations in parts of the world where secularization has gone furthest. John Paul II is not mistaken in recalling the central importance of the priestly task of mediation through prayer, sacrifice, and the ministry of the sacraments. While these sacred functions do not exhaust the whole nature of priesthood, they give a properly priestly tone to all the activities of the bishop and presbyter. Just as the career of Jesus reached its climax in the paschal mystery, so the activity of the ministerial priest culminates in the life of worship by which the church is brought into the mystery of Christ. However much importance we attach to other forms of ministry, it would be a mistake to forget that "the liturgy is the high point toward which the activity of the Church is directed and, at the same time, the source from which all its power flows" (SC 10). Because this is true, the liturgical ministry holds a preeminent and indispensable place in priestly existence.

IV. THE PASTORAL MINISTRY

W E HAVE SEEN THAT SOME THEOLOGIANS, in seeking to define ministerial priesthood, begin with the ministry of the word, the prophetic. To preach the gospel, they declare, is the first and foremost task. Catholic word-theologians, however, affirm that the word is efficacious and that it reaches its high point in the sacraments, and especially in the eucharist, in which the words of consecration effect the presence of the incarnate Word and his sacrificial action. This emphasis on the word narrows the gap between Catholics and Protestants—notably Lutherans, who look upon the sacraments as extensions of the word. But Catholic sacramental realism precludes a reductionist view that would treat sacraments as a mere form of the word, that is to say, as oriented only to the fostering of faith. Sacraments bring about a real encounter with the living Christ, who is present in them with his transforming power.

The Pastoral Responsibility of the Ordained

Theologians of a second school, following Thomas Aquinas and the Council of Trent, define the ministry primarily in terms of sacraments and worship. The ministry of the eucharist, they hold, is the function that is most specific to the ordained priest. But does this approach sufficiently emphasize that sacraments do not exist for their own sake? According to the medieval dictum,

45

sacraments are for the sake of people *(sacramenta propter homines)*. The ministry of the sacraments would be fruitless unless the people were nourished by them. Thus the sacramental interpretation of ministry calls for some consideration of the pastoral function.

The sacramental interpretation of priesthood, taken alone, fails to do justice to the priestly office of the bishop. Many medieval theologians taught that the presbyter has the fullness of the sacrament of order and that bishops receive through ordination only an increment of administrative power or jurisdiction.[1] Vatican II, returning to an earlier patristic position, which agrees with Eastern Orthodoxy, teaches that bishops have the fullness of the priesthood and that episcopal ordination is itself a grade of the sacrament of order. What is distinctive to the bishop is the pastoral office of presiding over the people of God. All bishops, provided that they are in hierarchical communion with the great church and the Holy See, are members of the episcopal college, which has collective responsibility for the teaching and government of the church as a whole. The majority of bishops are assigned to particular dioceses as chief pastors or auxiliaries.

LG 20, describing the office of bishop, gives primary emphasis to the task of shepherding the flock of Christ. It declares, for instance: "The bishops ... have undertaken, along with their assistants, the presbyters and deacons, the service of the community, presiding in place of God over the flock, whose shepherds they are, as teachers of doctrine, priests of sacred worship, and ministers of government." Note that in this statement the pastoral office is not identified exclusively with the ministry of government, but is seen as including this as one of its three functions.

If bishops have a higher degree of priestly ministry than presbyters, it follows that pastoral authority belongs to the concept of priesthood itself. The ministerial priesthood belongs especially to bishops but also to presbyters as associates of bishops under

Jesus Christ the chief shepherd. This is equivalently stated in LG 28 and PO 6.

Since Vatican II some excellent theologians have proposed theologies of priesthood that are centered on the role of pastor or shepherd. Walter Kasper, Jean Galot, and to some extent Hans Urs von Balthasar represent this perspective.

Kasper

Walter Kasper makes a clear and forthright proposal to get away from narrowly cultic concepts of priesthood. In an article for **Concilium** published in 1969 he begins with the concept of Jesus Christ as shepherd.[2] Christ, he holds, breaks through all cultic barriers, thereby transcending the distinction between the sacred and the profane and embodying in concrete form the universal saving love of God. To give an ecclesiological foundation to his proposal, Kasper speaks of the universal priesthood of the whole people of God, which is expressed in a great variety of charisms and ministries distributed by the Holy Spirit in the church. This variety, he points out, makes it necessary that there be a charism of administrative leadership, charged with the integration and coordination of all the charisms. In the New Testament, Kasper observes, the Christian leaders are designated not by sacral terms (such as *hiereus, sacerdos,* and *pontifex*) but rather by secular terms such as *episcopos* (supervisor), *prebyteros* (elder), and *diakonos* (servant). Using the New Testament as authority, Kasper maintains that the priestly office needs to be desacralized and demythologized. Kasper describes priestly office primarily in functional terms, as community leadership. But because the community is one of faith and worship, such leadership in his view necessarily involves the ministry of word and sacrament.

Even for Kasper, however, priesthood is more than functional. Because it is a service toward Christ, it reaches down and takes hold of the very depths of the priest's existence. He becomes what he does, one who lives for others as Christ did. To perform his tasks adequately the priest is endowed with certain charisms, especially those implied in the "indelible character" of the office. The sacramental character given in priestly ordination is for Kasper a permanent mission to service on behalf of others.

Within the broad function of community leadership, Kasper recognizes a plurality of particular functions, which he groups under the three traditional rubrics of ministry of the word, sacramental ministry, and fraternal service in a reciprocal ministry of love. In connection with this third function he emphasizes the importance of promoting inner-church unity. He advocates a "democratic" style of leadership that aims at the fullest possible collaboration and agreement. Autocratic leadership, he warns, becomes an occasion of strife and thereby fails in its task of integration.[3]

Galot

Another contemporary theologian who explains the meaning of priesthood primarily in terms of pastoral office is Jean Galot, a Belgian Jesuit teaching at the Gregorian University.[4] The priest, for him, is a shepherd called to feed the sheep of Christ and, if necessary, to lay down his life for them. The office of shepherd is not to be defined in opposition to the ministry of word and sacrament, but rather as including them. Pastoral leadership in the broad sense therefore extends beyond the function of governance, while including it. The three functions of preaching, worship, and community leadership become for Galot so many expressions of the shepherd's love. Like the Good Shepherd in the gospels, the priest must develop interpersonal relations with those committed to his care, just as Jesus knows his own and is known by them (Jn 10:14).

Jesus, according to Galot, entrusted the shepherding office to the Twelve. Bishops then succeeded to the office of the apostles, and presbyters share in that office. Priesthood, however, is not reducible to a mere charism of leadership. Priests have authority by reason of the office into which they enter. By sacramental ordination the priest is made a sharer in Christ's own pastoral office. The pastors par excellence are the bishops, who preside over the flock of Christ. The possession of pastoral office is what distinguishes ministerial priests from lay persons. Even though the laity may perform certain pastoral tasks, e.g., as parish administrators, they cannot hold the office of pastor unless and until they become priests.

Galot is not persuaded by those who want to define the priesthood solely or predominantly by the ministry of the word. This branch of ministry, he grants, has a certain priority in the sense that it is presupposed by the others. But it is incomplete until it reaches its culmination in the liturgy. Going beyond the liturgical, Galot warns against the views of Ivan Illich and other contemporary authors, who seem to him to be falling back into the narrowly cultic concept that would define priesthood in terms of ritual functions such as presidency at the eucharist. Such presidency, he points out, should not be isolated from the entire pastoral mission of the priest, under pain of mutilating the gospel notion of priesthood and returning to medieval ritualism.

The controlling notion in Galot's concept of priesthood is the formation of community. Priestly activity begins with missionary evangelization, which is a call to constitute a new community or to join a community to which one does not yet belong. Within the community, the priest must be an agent of growth and unity, objectives to be achieved through preaching, liturgical worship, and pastoral governance. In his prayer and sacrifice the priest, like Christ, intercedes with God on behalf of the human family.

Although Christ is rightly described as the sole mediator, Galot maintains that the priest may in some sense be called a mediator—one who carries on the task of mediation not in an independent way but by participation in the mediation of Christ. He represents the faithful in the sight of God, and God in the sight of human beings. As shepherd the priest is called to imitate the virtues and attitudes of Christ, reflecting Christ's pastoral countenance.

Galot does not limit the pastoral activity of priests to those who are formally installed as pastors. For him pastoral activity includes the work of missionaries, who go forth as Paul did to spread the word of God to populations that have not yet heard it. Within the community of faith pastoral activity may be shared by a team of priests collaboratively engaged in pastoral tasks. Just as bishops are by their ordination brought into a college, so priests are united among themselves by collegial bonds. The priests in a diocese constitute a single presbyterium, and all priests throughout the world are linked to one another in a close fraternity by reason of the sacred order and mission that they have received in common. All priests, whether diocesan or religious, are associated with the body of bishops and are called to labor for the good of the whole church (LG 28). The residential bishop is a sign and agent of unity for the diocese. As fellow-workers with their bishops, presbyters must strive to reconcile Catholics to one another, so that the church may be a more effective sign and instrument of that unity to which all the faithful are called in Christ.

Balthasar

Hans Urs von Balthasar, whose word-oriented concept of priesthood I have set forth in my third chapter, supplements this approach with another, which relies on the motif of the shepherd.[5] He points out the many passages in the gospels in which Jesus describes himself, or is described, as shepherd, a term already charged with rich resonances from the Old Testament. The image of the shepherd brings out the missionary aspect of the ministry of Jesus and of his commissioned disciples—their role as teachers and their function as rulers of the flock. Together with these two functions, the image connotes the sacrificial or sacerdotal dimension, inasmuch as the Good Shepherd lays down his life for the sheep.

In several key passages of the New Testament, Balthasar points out, those charged with the office of leadership are called pastors, and are exhorted to follow the example of Jesus, the chief shepherd. This image provides a basis for a rich priestly spirituality, as we shall see in our final chapter. The shepherd must be totally dedicated to the flock and be prepared to suffer in its defense. As we are told in 1 Peter 5:1–3, the shepherds in their willingness to serve must be examples to the flock. The image of the shepherd is capable of expressing both the authority of the pastor over the sheep and the loving union by which he and the flock are mutually united.

The Charism of Office

The authority of the priest does not come from the community. Rather than receiving authority through delegation from the people, the priest derives his power from the episcopate through ordination and canonical mission. Ultimately his authority comes from God through Jesus Christ by way of apostolic succession. Jesus Christ, of course, held his authority from heaven, not from any human community (cf. Mk 11:27–33).

The divine source of his authority does not give the priest the right to lord it over the flock. He is under strict obligation to adhere to the gospel, to be faithful to the church, and to serve the people of God. "It is required of stewards that they be found trustworthy" (1 Cor 4:2). The power of priesthood is entirely for the sake of service. To govern successfully the pastor has to win the goodwill of the congregation and to build up a sense of community among them. To gain their trust one must consult them, respect their competences, and welcome their cooperation.

It would be a grave mistake for the priest to rely only on his authority of office and to neglect the charisms that are needed for the proper exercise of that office. For the shepherding function the most important charisms would include those pertaining to human relationships: the ability to meet people, to enter into dialogue with them, and to direct and organize. Because of the complexity of most modern parishes it is more important now than ever for the priest to draw on the time and abilities of others, including those in the diaconate and lay ministries. He must be capable of recognizing the talents and limitations of other persons, of evoking their initiatives, of empowering the gifted, and of forming effective teams, while at the same time exercising the necessary vigilance to prevent disorders.

It is almost self-evident that the pastor should take advantage of all the skills that can be mustered from members of his congregation. Presumably they can give him needed assistance on matters such as law, finance, construction, maintenance, education, and music in which the priest may lack personal competence. In delegating responsibility he will have to let others exercise some degree of authority, but the unity of the church requires that ultimate authority, under God, rest in the pope, the bishops, and the pastors appointed by them.

Because of the shortage of priests the administration of parishes is being entrusted more and more to deacons, women religious, and lay persons. Questions are raised about whether and under what conditions such persons can be pastors and exercise jurisdiction. I do not propose to settle here any questions debated among canon lawyers.[6] I believe it is clear, however, that whereas only ordained priests can be pastors in the strict sense of the word, nonpriests can receive temporary or delegated jurisdiction and can participate in church government. The integrity of the pastoral office nevertheless requires that permanent and ordinary jurisdiction rest in the hands of the ordained. Otherwise there would be a danger of undermining the hierarchical structure of the church and lapsing into a merely cultic style of priestly ministry.

Evangelical Outreach

In our denominationally divided society, we tend to think of pastoral activity as limited to the care of the faithful and thus to ignore the outreach that the parish ought to have toward all who live in the area. John Paul II offers a corrective in ***Redemptoris missio,*** where he writes: "Especially in those areas where Christians are in a minority, priests must be filled with special missionary zeal and commitment. The Lord entrusts to them not only the pastoral care of the Christian community, but also and above all the evangelization of those of their fellow citizens who do not belong to Christ's flock."[7]

Since Paul VI's great exhortation on Evangelization in the Modern World, it seems clear that all the activities of the parish should be centered on evangelization as the church's central mission. Evangelization, broadly defined, includes the proclamation of the gospel to those who are afar and the nurturing of believers in the faith, so that they may more effectively understand and practice it.

A vital church is one that looks outward, spreading the good news and inviting others to join. It is not enough to evangelize those who come into our buildings; as bearers of the gospel, we must move into the neighborhoods and workplaces to evangelize. The United States bishops, in their national plan for evangelization, have called upon parish leaders, especially pastors, to understand their ministry in terms of this plan.[8] Many now speak of "evangelizing parishes." In the words of Patrick J. Brennan, "The parish or church that has lost this attitude of invitation and mission has become incestuous, closed in upon itself, or maintenance-oriented, concerned with maintaining the status quo."[9] It is normally necessary, but hardly sufficient, to have a good RCIA program. Evangelization should be a dimension of every parish organization, including those dedicated to religious education, liturgy, youth, social justice, and the like. An evangelizing parish will have a vigorous program for keeping in contact with inactive and alienated parishioners and for making unchurched persons feel welcome. Some parishes, I am told, have an annual "Come Home for Christmas" campaign.

Evangelical outreach can be conducted through a great variety of groups within the parish. One thinks in this connection of prayer groups, Bible study groups, book clubs, and other cultural activities. It might be possible to arrange concerts and sacred plays, to have groups to evaluate popular films and television shows. The parish school can be a very important vehicle for fostering and transmitting Catholic culture.

Secular Calling of Laity

In the contemporary world the parish cannot isolate itself from the great human problems of the day, including poverty, unemployment, health care, housing, and the relief of those who suffer from disasters in various countries. The danger is that the priest, seeking to give adequate attention to all these areas, will be pulled in too many directions, and will suffer from burnout or enfeeble his sense of a distinctively priestly mission. John Paul II has repeatedly addressed this problem, and I believe that his advice should be heeded. On several occasions he has rejected the idea that the ministerial priesthood should take on a more "secular" character and resemble more closely the ministry of the laity. On the contrary, he maintains, the activity of the priest must be a clear sign of his specific identity and mission. Priests must certainly share in the concern of all Christians for truth and justice, but as priests they must perform this service in the perspective of eternal salvation. The pope warns in particular against political partisanship. With an eye on the Latin American situation he declared, in a 1979 address to priests and religious at Mexico City: "You are priests and members of religious orders. You are not social directors, political leaders, or functionaries of a temporal power. So I repeat to you: Let us not pretend to serve the gospel if we try to 'dilute' our charism through an exaggerated interest in the broad field of temporal problems. Do not forget that temporal leadership can easily become a source of division, while the priest should be a sign and factor of unity, of brotherhood. The secular functions are the proper field of action of the laity, who ought to perfect temporal matters with a Christian spirit (AA 4)."[10] Here in the United States priests may run a risk of turning themselves into community organizers or social activists and neglecting the specifically religious dimension of their vocation.

While accepting the call of Vatican II to center the life of the priest on the pastoral mission, John Paul II insists on the distinction between the vocations of the priesthood and of the laity. The priest, he says, animates and supports the laity in the exercise of the common priesthood of the baptized, but his own ministry belongs to another order. He is ordained "to act in the name of Christ the head, to bring people into the new life made accessible by Christ, to dispense to them the mysteries—the word, forgiveness, the bread of life—to gather them into his body, to help them form themselves from within, and to act according to the saving plan of God."[11] Attempts to make the priest more like the laity, he says, are detrimental to the church. He appeals to the life and personality of St. John Vianney to illustrate how to safeguard the identity of the priest "in its vertical dimension."[12] This dimension, according to the pope, is being threatened by a growing secularization, by the neglect of spiritual discipline, and by a unilateral concern for the temporal and social aspects of the pastoral ministry.[13]

Ecumenical Ministry

One dimension of priesthood that has been insufficiently emphasized, in my opinion, is the ecumenical. The Second Vatican Council thrust the Catholic Church into the heart of the ecumenical movement, but the doctrine of the priesthood was not sufficiently reinterpreted in that light. From many books and articles on the subject, even since Vatican II, one gets the impression that the priest is a strictly denominational functionary, responsible only for the internal life of a single communion or a single parish. Taking the high-priestly prayer of Jesus as an inspiration, every priest should be consumed with zeal for the visible union of all who believe in Christ through the testimony of the disciples.

The prayer of the ministerial priest, who is ordained to worship in the person of the church, has special efficacy. This is especially true when he prays for unity while offering the holy sacrifice. When the opportunity offers itself, the priest should lead the congregation in celebrating the mass for Christian unity. This mass should be celebrated with confidence that the prayer of Jesus, which it recalls, is more than an empty dream.

The Ecumenical Directory of 1993 states that "the parish, as an ecclesial unity gathered around the Eucharist, should be and proclaim itself to be the place of authentic ecumenical witness. Thus a great task for the parish is to educate its members in the ecumenical spirit."[14] Efforts should be made to imbue parishioners with a truly ecumenical spirit, including a readiness to recognize and esteem all that is good in other Christian traditions. The Directory itself offers many suggestions for implementing this ideal. For instance, it should be possible to raise the ecumenical consciousness of the parish by observing the annual week of Prayer for Christian Unity. This octave could be an occasion for inviting a minister of another church to preach or participate in a prayer service or some other ecumenical event. It would also be possible in Holy Week to bring Christians of different denominations together to make the Stations of the Cross or to engage in meditations on the Seven Last Words.

Any number of other measures come to mind. All liturgical services themselves can have an ecumenical quality by their fidelity to scripture and early church tradition. Many of our most popular hymns were composed by Protestants and accent themes that belong to our common Christian heritage. Regular preaching can be oriented to overcome the prejudices and hostilities that have become ingrained in Catholics, as in other Christians, over the centuries. In religious education programs, the teaching of other Christian churches and ecclesial communities should be correctly and honestly presented. The results of national and international ecumenical dialogues may be suitably publicized and studied. Local dialogue groups may be established if the help of competent experts is available.

Priests can advance the cause of ecumenism by joining ministerial associations and councils of churches that are open to Protestants, Anglicans, and Orthodox. Depending on circumstances, it may be desirable to establish covenants between parishes of different denominational affiliations. In accordance with such covenants, the churches can collaborate for pastoral care; they can share ministry programs, training, and facilities. With or without formal covenants, ecumenical groups can come together for Bible study, for prayer in common, and for discussing social and cultural issues that are of common concern. Catholics should be motivated to cooperate with other Christians in bearing witness to Christian values, such as respect for human life, support for the dignity and stability of marriage, and regard for public decency. The Vatican II Decree on Ecumenism pointed out the ecumenical potential of cooperation among Christians for peace, justice, and the integrity of the environment. "Cooperation among all Christians," said the council, "vividly expresses the bond that already unites them, and sets in clearer light the features of Christ the Servant. ... Through such cooperation, all believers in Christ can easily learn to acquire a better knowledge and appreciation of one another, so as to make the road that leads to Christian unity more smooth" (UR 12; cf. John Paul II, *Ut unum sint,* 40).

The Ecumenical Directory lays down helpful norms for mixed marriages. The Catholic party should respect the conscience of the non-Catholic, but should also be ready and anxious to share the riches of Catholicism. An authentically ecumenical attitude does not prevent, but on the contrary requires, measures taken to support the Catholic party in his or her own faith, and to strive that the children should be brought up in the Catholic tradition. While the family may be encouraged to attend religious services together, it must be recognized that only in exceptional circumstances is it permitted for both spouses to receive holy communion together. They may never do so in a church whose ministries and sacraments are not acknowledged as valid by the Catholic Church.[15]

Conclusion

As I hope this chapter has indicated, the metaphor of shepherd, understood in broad terms that include the ministry of word and sacrament as well as pastoral government, is very serviceable. While bringing out the participation of the ministerial priest in the pastoral authority of Christ, this metaphor does not preclude the exercise of certain pastoral functions by members of the laity and by unordained religious. The word-centered concept of priesthood, without limiting the ministry of the word to bishops and presbyters, calls attention to the power and public authority conferred by priestly ordination. The worship-centered concept, without restricting worship to the ordained, brings out the cultic functions that are proper to them.

The problem of priestly identity cannot be adequately solved without attention to all of the three dimensions we have studied. As I said in my first chapter, the Thomistic concept of configuration to Christ through sacramental ordination illuminates the representative role of the priest. Through the sacrament of ordination the priest is enabled to share in a specific way in the many-faceted work of mediation by which Christ accomplished our redemption. By reason of his public persona, the priest is par excellence the man of God and of the church.

V. THE PRIEST AS DISCIPLE

IN THIS FINAL CHAPTER I should like to propose some reflections on priestly spirituality. My main contention will be that it is essential for the priest to be intimately united to Christ the high priest, and thus to be holy. Unless a high level of holiness is achieved, it will not be possible to preach and teach effectively, to preside fruitfully over the worship of the community, or to direct the people of God toward its appointed goal.

The Church as Holy

Let me begin by putting this in an ecclesiological context. As far as the New Testament is concerned, the overarching and unifying purpose of the church can be expressed in three words: to be holy. In the Letter to the Ephesians, for example, we read that Christ gave himself up for the church "that he might sanctify her, having cleansed her by the washing of water with the word, that he might present the Church to himself in splendor, without spot or wrinkle or any such thing, that she might be holy and without blemish" (Eph 5:25–27). The Letter to the Hebrews says that Christ suffered "in order to sanctify the people through his own blood" (Heb 13:12). The Apocalypse of John says likewise that Christ "has freed us from our sins by his blood" (Rev 1:5).

Because of what Christ has done for it, the church is described in the New Testament as a holy nation (1 Pet 2:9), a holy priesthood

(1 Pet 2:5), and a holy temple (Eph 2:21). These epithets pertain not only to the church as a whole, but to its individual members. Every believer is a temple in whom the Spirit dwells (1 Cor 6:19) and in whom the divine persons are pleased to make their home (Jn 14:23). Even before they were known as Christians, the members of the church were called "saints" (e.g., Acts 9:13, 32, 41; 26:10, 18; Rom 12:13; 1 Cor 1:2; 6:1, 2; Eph 4:12; Phil 1:1; 4:21, 22; Col 1:2, 4; Rev 13:7). Before their conversion they may have been children of wrath, driven by their disorderly passions, but through baptism they died to sin and took on new life in Christ (Eph 1:1–10).

The meaning of Christian holiness is clarified by descriptions contrasting the Christians with the pagans of the surrounding world. Writing to the Philippians, Paul describes them as "children of God without blemish in the midst of a crooked and perverse generation, among whom you shine as lights in the world, holding fast the word of life" (Phil 2:15–16). Before their conversion they may have indulged in vices such as anger, wrath, malice, slander, and foul talk (Col 3:8). But, thanks to the new nature they have received in Christ, they are now endowed with "compassion, kindness, lowliness, meekness, and patience" (Col 3:12).

Paul recognizes, of course, that there are individual failures, but he never ceases to insist on the normative ideal. To the Thessalonians he writes: "We beseech and exhort you in the Lord Jesus, that as you learned from us how you ought to live to please God, you do so more and more. ... For this is the will of God, your sanctification" (1 Thess 4:1–3). Sanctification is, so to speak, the "one thing necessary" (cf. Lk 10:42). The biblical authors would have agreed with Léon Bloy that there is only one real tragedy in life: not to have been a saint.

In writing to the Corinthians, Paul is very specific about what holiness demands: "Do not be deceived; neither male prostitutes, nor sodomites, nor thieves, nor the greedy, nor drunkards, nor revilers, nor robbers will inherit the kingdom of God. And such were some of you. But you were washed, you were sanctified, you were justified in the name of the Lord Jesus Christ and in the Spirit of our God" (1 Cor 6:9–11).

Building on texts such as these and on the creeds that express our belief in the "holy Church," Vatican II taught that the church "is holy in a way that can never fail" (LG 39). In several texts it emphasized holiness as the prime purpose of the church. For example, it declared in the Constitution on the Liturgy that "the sanctification of human beings and the glorification of God in Christ" are the goals toward which all other activities of the church are directed (SC 10). But at the same time the council was conscious of grave shortcomings. "It does not escape the Church," says the Pastoral Constitution on the Church in the Modern World, "how great a distance lies between the message she offers and the human weakness of those to whom the gospel is entrusted" (GS 43). According to the council, the actual conduct of believers in many cases must be said to conceal rather than reveal the authentic face of Christ (GS 19). For this reason the church, now as always, stands in need of penance and purification (LG 8; cf. UR 4, 6).

It might have been expected that this frank admission that the church was falling far short of its essential purpose would have provoked a vigorous movement of spiritual reform and renewal, but in fact the energies of the church were deflected in other directions. Scarcely conscious of sin, many neglected the sacrament of penance and reconciliation. The pursuit of holiness on the part of clergy, religious, and laity was sometimes subordinated to activism of various kinds. Confronted by the sexual revolution and confusion about ethical norms, Catholic preachers, teachers, and parents hardly dared to explain the basic precepts of the moral law. The faithful have not infrequently been scandalized by reports of misconduct among clergy and religious, even among bishops. Evangelical Christians and Muslims are attracting great numbers of converts partly because they insist on higher moral standards than Catholics commonly do.

Recognizing the present crisis of holiness, the Extraordinary Synod of 1985 called for a profound conversion of heart, so that the church might stand forth as a sign and instrument of holiness. Saintly men and women, said the synod, have always been the primary source of renewal in the church. There is a great need today for saints as heralds of the gospel. Priests, who represent the church in an official and public manner, must be examples and promoters of holiness.

Jesus as Exemplar

The New Testament, I believe, offers precious resources for a recovery of priestly spirituality. One could begin with the portrayal of priesthood in the fifth and seventh chapters of Hebrews. Here we are told that the priest is someone chosen to act on behalf of people in relation to God (5:1); that he must offer up prayers and supplications (5:7), making intercession for others who draw near to God (7:25). The priest, encompassed by weakness, must be able to deal gently with the ignorant and the wayward (5:2), offering sacrifices for his own sins and those of others (5:3), and learning obedience by the experience of suffering (5:8). In Jesus we have a high priest who is supremely holy, blameless, untainted by sin (7:26). If the ministerial priesthood is a participation in that of Christ, it will have to reflect the qualities I have mentioned.

The biblical image of the Good Shepherd has rich potential as a basis of priestly spirituality. The shepherd, as the gospels tell us, must have a deep love for the sheep, know them intimately, lead them toward good pastures, defend them against ravenous wolves or roaring lions, and go out to search for those who stray from the fold. The First Epistle of Peter exhorts presbyters to imitate the Chief Shepherd. Three faults are particularly reprimanded: to labor under constraint rather than voluntarily; to be motivated by desire for profit rather than offering one's services freely; to domineer over the flock rather than being an example to them (1 Pet 5:1–3).

Conscious of the great trust that he was to place in the apostolic ministry, Jesus did not confer that responsibility lightly. Luke tells us that he prayed all night before choosing the Twelve from a larger band of disciples (Lk 6:12). Then he subjected them to a rigorous formation lasting over several years, making them sharers of his life, explaining his parables to them, answering their questions, challenging their assumptions, sending them forth on mission, and reviewing with them the results of their apostolic ventures.

Priestly ministry as we find it in the gospels is not just a job, a profession requiring a limited number of hours on duty, with a steady salary and assured periods of rest and recreation. Although time must be made for prayer and silence, the vocation is a total one, so that the priest is always in some sense on duty.

The apostolic calling involves two inseparable dimensions: being with Jesus and being sent forth. These two aspects are indicated by Mark's account of the choosing of the Twelve: "He appointed twelve to be with him and to be sent out to preach and have authority to cast out demons" (Mk 3:14). They must be with Jesus for the sake of their own conversion, which involves learning what he has to teach, acquiring his mentality, his style of existence and thinking; but they must also go forth so as to meet the spiritual needs of others, wherever the demands of the church's mission require.

Speaking of the formation of future priests, Vatican II in its Decree on Priestly Formation says that spiritual instruction should be imparted in such a way "that the students may learn to live in holy, familiar, and attentive union with the Father, through his Son Jesus Christ in the Holy Spirit. As they are to be conformed into the likeness of Christ the Priest by sacred ordination, they should also learn to cling to him by a close sharing of their whole life as friends" (OT 12). In speaking of this friendship with

Christ, the council no doubt has in mind the statement of Jesus to his apostles: "No longer do I call you servants, for the servant does not know what his master is doing; but I have called you friends, for all that I have heard from my Father I have made known to you. You did not choose me, but I chose you and appointed you that you should go and bear fruit and that your fruit should abide" (Jn 15:15–16).

The existential relationship of the ministerial priest to Jesus Christ is strongly emphasized by John Paul II. In his apostolic exhortation on priestly formation, *Pastores dabo vobis* (1992), he meditates on the Johannine account of the two disciples of John the Baptist who came to Jesus and stayed all day in his company in order to satisfy their quest for the Lamb of God. For any authentic vocation, the pope concludes, a real personal union with Christ is necessary. The priest must abide in Christ, so that Christ may abide in him and enable him to bear fruit, for apart from him the disciple can do nothing (Jn 15:4–5; cf. PDV 36).

The requirement of holiness in the apostolic ministry is powerfully brought out in the high-priestly prayer of Jesus at the Last Supper. Pleading with the Father for the companions he was sending into the world, Jesus says: "I do not pray that thou shouldst take them out of the world, but that thou shouldst keep them from the evil one. ... Sanctify them in the truth. ... And for their sake I sanctify *(hágiazō)* myself, that they also may be sanctified *(hēgiasménoi)* in truth" (Jn 17:15–19; RSV modified).

The final chapter of John's gospel emphasizes again the indissoluble conjunction between ministerial office and personal holiness. Before being invested with responsibility to feed the flock of Christ, Peter is required to answer three times the question whether he excels in love for Jesus. Satisfied with Peter's humble replies, Jesus gives him the pastoral charge, but only with the twice-repeated admonition, "Follow me" (Jn 21:19, 22). These words, echoing the call with which Peter's vocation began (Mt

4:19 parallel), now convey a call to martyrdom in the footsteps of the Master.

Although the call to faithful discipleship extends to all Christians, it comes with special urgency to those who enter holy orders. In the ordination rite the bishop reminds the candidate for the presbyterate of what the eucharist must mean for him: "You must carry out your mission of sanctifying in the power of Christ. Your ministry will perfect the spiritual sacrifice of the faithful by uniting it to Christ's sacrifice, the sacrifice which is offered sacramentally through your hands. Know what you are doing and imitate the mystery you celebrate. In the memorial of the Lord's death and resurrection, make every effort to die to sin and to walk in the new life of Christ." At the very moment when the sacrament of ordination is conferred, the bishop prays: "Almighty Father, grant to this servant of yours the dignity of the priesthood. Renew within him the spirit of holiness. As a co-worker with the order of bishop may he be faithful to the ministry that he receives from you, Lord God, and be to others a model of right conduct."

From these prayers two things seem evident; first, that the priest, by reason of ordination, receives the graces needed to achieve the holiness required by his office, and second, that the required holiness cannot be achieved without personal effort. We are reminded, therefore, of Paul's exhortations to Timothy: "Do not neglect the gift you have, which was given you by prophetic utterance when the elders laid their hands upon you" (1 Tim 4:14). And again: "I remind you to rekindle the gift of God that is within you through the laying on of my hands" (2 Tim 1:6). Priestly holiness is both a gift and a task. If we neglect the task, the gift will not profit us. Without personal holiness it will be possible to hold the office of a priest, and to minister the sacraments validly, but the fruitfulness of the ministry will be compromised.

Prayer and Sacraments

As a spiritual leader of the people of God, the ministerial priest has particular responsibilities in the realms of prayer and sacramental life. A priest who does not pray would be simply a contradiction in terms. The prayer of the priest in many ways resembles that of every other Christian, but the laity are entitled to look to the priest as one who may be presumed to have experience in the life of prayer, and the ability to counsel others in their perplexities. Sad to say, many of the faithful do not feel that the priests they know are qualified to direct them in the interior life. Too many priests give the appearance of being too busy and too involved in day-to-day business to take time for contemplation and spiritual direction.

In some respects the prayer of the priest differs from that of the laity. The priest prays as a public person, having a certain responsibility for the corporate life of the church. He is expected to make intercession for others, bringing their needs before the throne of grace. This he does to a great extent by engaging in liturgical prayer, that is to say, in the public prayer of the church as such. The Liturgy of the Hours is especially entrusted to priests, who are bound by their office to recite it. The psalter contains a rich treasury of prayers that were chanted by the assembly of Israel even before the time of Christ. Today the psalter can be reread in a christological and ecclesiological light. Some of the prayers are appropriately recited in the name of Christ, others in the name of the church or individuals or groups who may be in a situation to address God in the language given.

Prayer is never a merely human activity. In prayer, as John Paul II writes, "the true protagonist is God."[1] Our prayer becomes genuine and vital to the extent that we allow God to be present in it. Such prayer is a remedy for lassitude and discouragement. It reminds us of the goodness of creation and of the benefits of God's redemptive action, including his victory over sin and death. It orients us in hope toward the life to come. Prayer is therefore a source of spiritual peace and joy, an antidote to despondency and fear.

The fourth part of the *Catechism of the Catholic Church,* devoted to the theme of prayer, contains many useful suggestions for fostering the priest's own union with God and helping him instruct others in the ways of prayer. The analysis of the seven petitions of the Our Father shows how intimately connected this prayer is with the personal prayer of Jesus, as found in the seventeenth chapter of John's gospel.

Praying for the church, the priest remembers all who may be in special need—those tried by pain and suffering, the sick and the dying, those suffering temptation or enslaved by the power of sin. He prays likewise for those who exhibit goodwill and bring forth fruits of sanctity. He prays in a special way for the pope, the bishops, fellow priests, and parishioners.

The sacramental and liturgical ministry of the priest is an extension of his life of prayer. The ministry of penance and reconciliation gives him an opportunity to pray with and for sinners who are seeking to overcome the evil in their lives. The good confessor is one who makes good use of the sacrament of penance, which he receives in solidarity with the whole church penitent. The ecclesial and corporate dimensions of the sacrament of penance bring out the indispensable role of the priest as the official representative of the church.

Recognizing that in our time the faithful do not always hasten in great numbers to the confessional, Pope John Paul II calls upon priests to develop a pastoral strategy of the sacrament of reconciliation. They must remind Christians of the need to have a personal relationship with God and must arouse in them a sense of sin and a desire to receive the assurance of forgiveness through the ministry of the church.[2]

Most of all, the priest will center his devotional life on the eucharist, the sacrament that according to Vatican II contains in itself "the whole spiritual treasure of the Church." This sacrament, says the council, is the center of the gathering of faithful over which the priest presides (PO 5). The whole life of the priest can be an effort to carry into his conduct the action of Christ that is celebrated in the eucharistic sacrifice (cf. PO 14). Recognizing the awesome mystery, the priest will strive to prepare adequately before saying mass, and throughout his day he will aspire to remain close to Christ by visits to the blessed sacrament and other eucharistic devotions, which, as I have said, are not contrary to the spirit and teaching of Vatican II.

Discipleship

Although the disciples in the lifetime of Jesus were not yet priests in the full sense of the word, many contemporary authors are applying to priests the ideals of the evangelical life set forth in the gospel descriptions of the community of the disciples. Raymond Brown, for example, explains that the spiritual idealism of the later Christian priesthood has been powerfully shaped by the role of the disciple as graphically depicted in the gospels.[3] Ministerial priests have a sense of being formed in a special way by the demands of Christian discipleship. Whereas the priesthood in the Old Testament came by birth, the priest of the New Testament must receive a call, a vocation, so absolute and radical that it permits no competitive concern or diversion. No one can serve two masters (Mt 6:24); those who aspire to be disciples of Jesus must be prepared to leave father and mother, wife and children, for the sake of the kingdom of God (Lk 14:26; cf. Mt 10:37). No other obligation, even that of burying a beloved father, is allowed to interfere with the demands of discipleship (Mt 8:21–22; Lk 9:59–60). When one has embarked on the path of discipleship, there can be no turning back. "No one who has put his hand to the plow and looks back is fit for the kingdom of God" (Lk 9:62). The radicalism of the gospel, according to John

Paul II, is expressed by evangelical counsels.[4] The three standard
counsels of obedience, poverty, and chastity, though they apply
in a stricter sense to the consecrated life of the vowed religious,
are also applicable in some sense to diocesan priests. Some
priests, of course, are consecrated to God by the public profession of the evangelical counsels in some form of religious institute. In his recent apostolic exhortation, *Vita consecrata,* John
Paul II teaches that "the sacrament of holy orders finds a particular fruitfulness in this consecration, inasmuch as it fosters a
closer union with the Lord. ... In the priest, in fact, the vocation to
the priesthood and the vocation to the consecrated life converge
in a profound and dynamic unity."[5]

Every priest at his ordination promises obedience to his
bishop. Such obedience is apostolic, since it is related to the hierarchical structure of the church; it is collegial in the sense of
being lived out in solidarity with the presbyterate, and is pastoral,
insofar as it is devoted to the good of the flock.

The poverty of the priest requires a responsible use of material
goods and an ability to relinquish them with interior freedom for
the sake of better fulfilling God's redemptive plan. Every priest
keeps before his eyes the example of Christ who became poor out
of love for us (2 Cor 8:9), who had no place to lay his head (Lk
9:58), and who instructed those who would be perfect to give all
their worldly possessions to the poor (Mt 19:21 parallel).
Aspirants to the priesthood are to be trained in such a way "that
they will readily renounce things that may be lawful but not
expedient, and learn to conform themselves to Christ crucified"
(OT 9). According to canon law, clerics are to cultivate a simple
style of life and avoid whatever has a semblance of vanity; they
should donate any superfluous goods to charitable causes (CIC,
can. 282). Such an attitude of poverty ensures that the priest is
available to be sent wherever his work is needed, going, as did
the first missionaries, without traveling bag or visible means of
support (cf. Mt 10:8–10). By their freedom from attachment to

riches, the priestly body can erect a sign that contradicts the excessive trust in money and material security that is one of the characteristic aberrations of our time.

Celibacy

Priestly celibacy as a counsel goes back to the New Testament. Jesus, himself celibate, commended those who made themselves eunuchs for the sake of the kingdom of heaven (Mt 19:12). Paul was apparently celibate and recommended that state for the sake of a more undivided dedication to the service of the Lord (1 Cor 7:32). Over the centuries the Catholic Church has been well served by celibate priests. In its Decree on Priestly Formation (OT 10) Vatican II reiterated the teaching of Trent and Pius XII that consecrated chastity is, objectively speaking, a more blessed state than marriage although, of course, all are bound to seek perfection in the state to which they as individuals are called. In its Decree on the Ministry and Life of Priests (PO 16), the council gave many reasons for regarding the celibate life as appropriate for priests. Among other considerations it mentioned that the celibate condition reflects the mysterious union between Christ and the church. The celibate priest can more fittingly represent Christ in his nuptial relationship to the church, which, as we have seen, is displayed in every celebration of the eucharist.

Where there is a high degree of faith and commitment to the following of Christ, celibate vocations will be plentiful. Celibacy commends itself to those who take seriously the call of Jesus to leave everything and follow him even to the cross. The clamor for a married clergy and for temporary ordinations comes predominantly from quarters in which the radicalism of the gospel has been diluted.

It would be dogmatically possible for the Catholic Church to relax the requirement of priestly celibacy, but in my judgment such a development would be an impoverishment of Catholic

life. It would have unfortunate repercussions regarding the apostolic availability of priests and their pastoral relationship to the
faithful. The Second Vatican Council, the recent popes, and the
Synod of 1990 have all strongly supported the discipline of
celibacy in the Latin rite. The recent synod declared that "it does
not wish to leave any doubts in the mind of anyone regarding the
Church's firm will to maintain the law that demands perpetual
and freely chosen celibacy for the present and future candidates
for priestly ordination in the Latin rite."[6]

Raymond Brown, in his ***Priest and Bishop,*** has several apposite
observations on this question. He points out that while celibacy was
not required of all who followed Jesus, or even of the Twelve, it was
held up as an ideal to those who were able to bear it. Since this ideal
was proposed precisely for the sake of the kingdom, it is not sur-
prising that from a very early period the church began to seek candidates who were willing to serve as celibate priests. Brown
contends further that since the witness of celibacy is conspicuously
lacking in many other Christian churches, the Roman Catholic
Church has an ecumenical duty to bear an effective witness on this
score. "Perhaps," he writes, "this would be possible without a law,
but one must admit that it is the law of priestly celibacy that makes
it clear that those who accept it are doing it for the sake of Christ
and not simply because they prefer to be bachelors."[7]

In short, celibacy in the service of the gospel makes sense as a
sign that Christ makes a claim on the whole person of those
whom he calls to represent him publicly and through whom he
acts as head of the church. Objections to the institution of
celibacy are frequently connected with more fundamental errors
concerning the theology of the priesthood.

Conclusion

Although all the baptized are called to holiness, that call
comes with special urgency to the priest, who represents Jesus

the sinless one. Keeping his eyes fixed on Christ, the priest will unceasingly strive to be able to say with Paul, "Be imitators of me, as I am of Christ" (1 Cor 11:1). In the full sense of the word, Christ alone is holy because all other holiness is a participation in his. As Son of God, uniquely filled with the Holy Spirit, he is the pattern of all priestly holiness. As they grow in love for him, priests will rejoice in their vocation and will experience that his yoke is easy and his burden light (cf. Mt 11:30).

NOTES

I. The Priest and the Church

[1]Hans Küng, *Why Priests?* (Garden City, N.Y.: Doubleday, 1972).

[2]"Vatican Declaration on Hans Küng," *Origins* 4 (March 6, 1975): 577, 579.

[3]Edward Schillebeeckx, *Ministry: Leadership in the Community of Jesus Christ* (New York: Crossroad, 1981), 72–73, 138–39.

[4]Congregation for the Doctrine of the Faith, Letter to Bishops, "The Minister of the Eucharist," *Origins* 13 (September 15, 1983): 229–33. For further discussion of Schillebeeckx's *Ministry* see the review of Walter Kasper in *Communio: International Catholic Review* 10 (Summer 1983): 185–95 and those of Albert Vannoye and Henri Crouzel in *The Clergy Review* 68 (May 1983): 155–74.

[5]Congregation for the Doctrine of the Faith, Letter to Edward Schillebeeckx, "Who Can Preside at the Eucharist?" *Origins* 14 (January 24, 1985): 523, 525.

[6]See Pierre Grelot, *Eglise et ministères* (Paris: Cerf, 1983), 134.

[7]Thomas Aquinas, *Summa theologiae*, Part III, qu. 63, art. 3.

[8]Daniel Donovan, *What Are They Saying about Ministerial Priesthood?* (New York: Paulist, 1992), 39, summarizing Congar's critique of the Abbé Germain Long-Hasselmans in *Revue des sciences religieuses* 25 (1951): 187–99, 270–304, esp. 288–301.

[9]The *Nota explicativa praevia* appended to the Vatican II Constitution on the Church stated in its second paragraph that episcopal consecration confers an "ontological participation in sacred functions" (*ontologica participatio sacrorum munerum*), and then distinguished

the functions (*munera*) from powers (*potestates*). I take this as implying that the character is in some sense entitative, not simply operative.

[10]In suggesting that the character is a *habitus* I follow Alexander of Hales and Bonaventure. Thomas Aquinas, holding with Aristotle that a *habitus* cannot be indifferent to being well or badly used, preferred to classify the character as a "spiritual power" (*spiritualis potestas*) within the genus of quality. See his *Summa theologiae*, Part III, qu. 63, art. 2.

[11]Bernard D. Marliangeas, *Clés pour une théologie du Ministère: In persona Christi, in persona Ecclesiae* (Paris: Beauchesne, 1978), 138. Yves Congar's preface to this work is especially insightful. Among the many treatments of this theme in English one may mention David N. Power, "Representing Christ in Community and Sacrament," in *Being a Priest Today*, ed. Donald J. Goergen (Collegeville, Minn.: Liturgical Press, 1992), 97–123.

[12]Daniel Pilarczyk, "Defining the Priesthood," *Origins* 20 (October 18, 1990): 297–300, at 299.

II. The Ministry of the Word

[1]See Council of Trent, Session 5, chap. 2, n. 9, in Norman Tanner, ed., *Decrees of the Ecumenical Councils* 2:669. See also Session 24, canon 4, in Tanner 2:763.

[2]Karl Rahner, "Priest and Poet," *Theological Investigations* 3 (Baltimore: Helicon, 1967), 307.

[3]Ibid., 313.

[4]Karl Rahner, "The Point of Departure in Theology for Determining the Nature of the Priestly Office," *Theological Investigations* 12 (New York: Seabury/Crossroad, 1974), 36.

[5]Karl Rahner, "The Word and the Eucharist," *Theological Investigations* 4 (Baltimore: Helicon, 1966), 260.

[6]Ibid., 263.

[7]Ibid., 281.

[8]Rahner, "Point of Departure," *Theological Investigations* 12:35.

[9]Hans Urs von Balthasar, "The Priest of the New Covenant," *Explorations in Theology IV. Spirit and Institution* (San Francisco: Ignatius, 1995), 353–81.

[10]Joseph Ratzinger, *The Open Circle: The Meaning of Christian*

Brotherhood (New York: Sheed & Ward, 1966). German original 1959.

[11]Joseph Ratzinger, *Theological Highlights of Vatican II* (New York: Paulist, 1966), 175–78.

[12]Ibid., 176–77.

[13]Joseph Ratzinger, "Zur Frage nach dem Sinn des priesterlichen Dienstes," *Geist und Leben* 41 (1968): 347–76. An English translation with the title "Priestly Ministry: A Search for Its Meaning" appeared in *Emmanuel* 76 (1970): 442–53, 490–505.

[14]Joseph Ratzinger, "Biblical Foundations of Priesthood," *Origins* 20 (October 18, 1990): 310–14, at 312.

[15]Paul VI, Apostolic Exhortation *Evangelii nuntiandi* §2 (Washington, D.C.: United States Catholic Conference, 1976), p. 6.

[16]See the Apostolic Exhortation on the Laity, *Christifideles laici*; text in *Origins* 18 (February 9, 1989): 561–95.

[17]*Fulfilled in Your Hearing* (Washington, D.C.: United States Catholic Conference, 1982, reprinted 1995), 15.

III. The Ministry of Worship

[1]John Paul II, Holy Thursday Letter *Dominicae cenae* §2; text in Edward Kilmartin, *Church, Eucharist, and Priesthood* (New York: Paulist, 1981), 71. In a footnote the pope refers to the Council of Trent as authority for his statement on the institution of the sacramental priesthood. In instances such as this the church does not intend to settle historical-critical questions about the mind of the biblical author but to answer the religious question about the implications of the text for the life of the faithful. In this connection see Raymond E. Brown's article, "Hermeneutics," in the *New Jerome Biblical Commentary* (Englewood Cliffs, N.J.: Prentice Hall, 1990), 1146–65, at 1163.

[2]Quotations from Luther in Joseph Ratzinger, *Principles of Catholic Theology* (San Francisco: Ignatius, 1987), 261–62.

[3]Leonardo Boff, *Ecclesiogenesis: The Base Communities Reinvent the Church* (Maryknoll, N.Y.: Orbis, 1986), 70.

[4]See the Notification on Boff's book, *Church: Charism and Power* (New York: Crossroad, 1985) in *Origins* 14 (April 4, 1985): 683–87, at 686.

[5]I do not here wish to enter into the question of the sacramental powers of Protestant ministers whose orders are not recognized by the Catholic Church as standing within the apostolic succession. Some years ago I addressed this topic in "The Protestant Minister and the Prophetic Mission," *Theological Studies* 21 (1960): 544–80. See the reflections of Maurice Villain in his article "Can There Be Apostolic Succession Outside the Chain of Imposition of Hands?" *Concilium* 34, *Apostolic Succession: Rethinking a Barrier to Unity* (New York: Paulist, 1968), 87–104.

[6]Ratzinger, Principles of Catholic Theology, 293.

[7]See Otto Semmelroth, "The Priestly People of God and Its Official Ministers" in *Concilium* 31, *The Sacraments in General* (New York: Paulist, 1968), 87–100.

[8]In his excellent study of the terms *in persona Christi* and *in persona Ecclesiae* Bernard D. Marliangeas somewhat neglects the application of these terms beyond the eucharistic action. See his *Clés pour une théologie du ministère* (Paris: Beauchesne, 1978).

[9]The Greek "en prosōpō Christou" is translated in the RSV "in the presence of Christ."

[10]John Paul II, "Apostolic Exhortation on Reconciliation and Penance" §29; *Origins* 14 (December 20, 1984): 432–58, at 450.

[11]Robert Sokolowski, *Eucharistic Presence: A Study in the Theology of Disclosure* (Washington, D.C.: Catholic University of America, 1994).

[12]Pius XII, *On the Sacred Liturgy (Mediator Dei)*, 69 (New York: America Press, 1948), 38, quoting St. John Chrysostom, *In Joann. Hom.*, 86:4. Cf. Sokolowski, *Eucharistic Presence*, 15.

[13]Cf. Thomas Aquinas, *Summa theologiae*, Part III, qu. 82, art. 1.

[14]Cf. Council of Trent, Session XXII, chap. 2; DS 1743.

[15]I am here following the insightful observations of Peter Casarella in his review article, "Questioning the Primacy of Method: On Sokolowski's *Eucharistic Presence*," *Communio* 22 (Winter 1995): 668–701.

[16]Pius XII, Encyclical *Mediator Dei* §87 (New York: America Press, 1948), 44.

[17]Eamon Duffy, "The Stripping of the Altars and the Liturgy: Some

Reflections on a Modern Dilemma," *Antiphon 1* (Spring 1996): 2–4, at 3.

[18]John Paul II, *Dominicae cenae* §3, pp. 72–73.

IV. The Pastoral Ministry

[1]St. Thomas, influenced by Peter Lombard, held in his early work that episcopal ordination is not a sacrament and that, unlike presbyteral ordination, it does not confer an indelible character. See the texts cited in Avery Dulles, *A Church to Believe In* (New York: Crossroad, 1983), 160–61, and the corresponding footnotes.

[2]Walter Kasper, "A New Dogmatic Outlook on the Priestly Ministry," *Concilium* 43, *The Identity of the Priest* (New York: Paulist, 1969), 20–33.

[3]Ibid., 32.

[4]Jean Galot, *Theology of the Priesthood* (San Francisco: Ignatius, 1984), esp. chap. 7, "The Nature of Priestly Ministry," 129–53.

[5]Hans Urs von Balthasar, "The Priest of the New Covenant," in his *Explorations in Theology IV. Spirit and Institution* (San Francisco: Ignatius, 1995), 353–81, esp. 365–81.

[6]On this issue see the remarks of James H. Provost in *The Code of Canon Law: A Text and Commentary* (New York: Paulist, 1985), 164–65 and those of John E. Lynch, ibid., 204. The question is sharpened by Aurelie A. Hagstrom, "Can Lay People Govern the Church?" *America* 174 (February 17, 1996): 20–21 and Ladislas Orsy, "Lay Persons in Church Governance? A Disputed Question," *America* 174 (April 6, 1996): 10–13.

[7]John Paul II, Encyclical *Redemptoris missio* §67; text in *Origins* 20 (January 31, 1991): 541–68, at 560.

[8]United States Bishops, "Go and Make Disciples: A National Plan and Strategy for Catholic Evangelization in the United States," *Origins* 22 (December 3, 1992): 423–32.

[9]Patrick J. Brennan, *The Evangelizing Parish: Theologies and Strategies for Renewal* (Allen, Texas: Tabor, 1987), p. 18.

[10]John Paul II, "A Vision of the Priest's Role," *Origins* 8 (February 15, 1979): 547–49, at 548–49.

[11]John Paul II, "The Example of St. John Vianney," *Origins* 15 (April 3, 1986): 685–91, at 689.

[12]Ibid.

[13]Ibid., 686.

[14]"The 1993 Directory for Ecumenism," §67; *Origins* 23 (July 29, 1993): 129–60, at 141.

[15]For the current discipline of the Catholic Church on eucharistic sharing see ibid., §§ 125, 130, 131, 132, and 160; pp. 148, 150.

V. The Priest as Disciple

[1]John Paul II, *Crossing the Threshold of Hope* (New York: Knopf, 1994), 17.

[2]John Paul II, "The Example of St. John Vianney" §7; text in *Origins* 15 (April 3, 1986): 685–91, at 688.

[3]Raymond E. Brown, *Priest and Bishop: Biblical Reflections* (New York: Paulist, 1970), 21–26.

[4]John Paul II, Apostolic Exhortation *Pastores dabo vobis* §§27–30 (Washington, D.C.: United States Catholic Conference, 1992), pp. 71–81.

[5]John Paul II, Apostolic Exhortation *Vita consecrata* §30; text in *Origins* 25 (April 4, 1996): 681–719, at 691.

[6]Synod of 1990, Proposition 11; quoted in John Paul II, *Pastores dabo vobis* §29, pp. 76–77. See also Paul VI, Encyclical *Sacerdotalis caelibatus* of June 24, 1967; trans. in Austin Flannery, ed., *Vatican Council II: More Postconciliar Documents* (Northport, N.Y.: Costello, 1982), 285–317.

[7]Brown, *Priest and Bishop*, 26. For the postbiblical history of the rule of celibacy see Alfons Maria Stickler, *The Case for Clerical Celibacy* (San Francisco: Ignatius, 1995).

INDEX OF NAMES